FREEDOM OF THE PRESS 2003

FREEDOM OF THE PRESS 2003

A Global Survey of Media Independence

Edited by Karin Deutsch Karlekar

WITH ESSAYS BY
LEONARD R. SUSSMAN,
RONALD KOVEN, AND
THOMAS A. DINE

FREEDOM HOUSE
NEW YORK ▪ WASHINGTON, D.C.

ROWMAN & LITTLEFIELD PUBLISHERS, INC.
LANHAM ▪ BOULDER ▪ NEW YORK ▪ TORONTO ▪ OXFORD

ROWMAN & LITTLEFIELD PUBLISHERS, INC.

Published in the United States of America
by Rowman & Littlefield Publishers, Inc.
A wholly owned subsidary of The Rowman & Littlefield Publishing Group, Inc.
4501 Forbes Boulevard, Suite 200, Lanham, MD 20706
www.rowmanlittlefield.com

P.O. Box 317, Oxford OX2 9RU, United Kingdom

British Library Cataloguing in Publication Information Available

Library of Congress Cataloging-in-Publication Data Available

ISBN 0-7425-2873-1 (cloth : alk. paper)
ISBN 0-7425-2874-X (pbk. : alk. paper)

Printed in the United States of America

⊖™ The paper used in this publication meets the minimum requirements of
American National Standard for Information Sciences—Permanence of Paper for
Printed Library Materials, ANSI/NISO Z39.48-1992.

Table of Contents

Acknowledgments

Freedom of the Press 2003 could not have been completed without the contributions of numerous Freedom House staff and consultants. Freedom House would like to thank the Freedom Forum, the World Press Freedom Committee, and Bette Bao Lord for their generous contributions towards our ongoing work to promote freedom of expression. Additional support for this year's survey was provided by The Lynde and Harry Bradley Foundation, the Lilly Endowment, and the F. M. Kirby Foundation.

This year's survey was written by Karin Deutsch Karlekar, Peter Doran, Jeff Moorhead, Leonard R. Sussman, and Michael Goldfarb. Freedom House would also like to thank Ronald Koven, European representative of the World Press Freedom Committee, and Thomas A. Dine, president of Radio Free Europe/Radio Liberty, for their contributions.

We are grateful for the insights provided by those who served on this year's review team, including Freedom House staff members Jennifer Windsor, Adrian Karatnycky, Arch Puddington, Leonard R. Sussman, and Amanda Schnetzer, as well as Marilyn Greene of the World Press Freedom Committee and Whayne Dillehay of the International Center for Journalists. In addition, the ratings and narratives were reviewed by a number of regional and country analysts, including Martin Edwin Andersen and Michael Gold-Biss (Latin America), Edward McMahon and Cindy Shiner (Africa), Gary Gambill and Mikaela McDermott (Middle East and North Africa), Charles Graybow (Asia), and Aili Piano and

Christine Nelson (Eurasia). This report also reflects the findings of the Freedom House study *Freedom in the World 2003: The Annual Survey of Political Rights and Civil Liberties.*

Karin Deutsch Karlekar, a senior researcher at Freedom House, served as managing editor of this year's survey. Overall guidance for the project was provided by Amanda Schnetzer, director of studies, and by Arch Puddington, director of research. Peter Doran and Jeff Moorhead participated in all stages of the report's preparation. Additional assistance was provided by Christina Hartman, Amy Phillips, and Renee Manuel. Anne Green, of Greenways Graphic Design, was responsible for the design and layout of the book, while Linda Stern served as the principal copy editor.

Survey Methodology

This survey of 193 countries expands a process conducted since 1980 by Freedom House. The findings are widely used by governments, academics, and the news media in many countries. The degree to which each country permits the free flow of information determines the classification of its media as "Free," "Partly Free," or "Not Free." Countries scoring 0 to 30 are regarded as having "Free" media; 31 to 60, "Partly Free" media; and 61 to 100, "Not Free" media. The criteria for such judgments and the arithmetic scheme for displaying the judgments are described below. Assigning numerical points allows for comparative analysis among the countries surveyed as well as facilitating an examination of trends over time.

Criteria

This study is based on universal criteria. The starting point is the smallest, most universal unit of concern: the individual. We recognize cultural differences, diverse national interests, and varying levels of economic development. Yet Article 19 of the Universal Declaration of Human Rights holds that:

> Everyone has the right to freedom of opinion and expression; this right includes freedom to hold opinions without interference and to seek, receive, and impart information and ideas through any media regardless of frontiers.

The operative word for this survey is *everyone*. All states, from the most democratic to the most authoritarian, are committed to this doctrine through the UN system. To deny that doctrine is to deny the universality of information freedom—a basic human right. We recognize that cultural distinctions or economic underdevelopment may limit the volume of news flows within a country, but these and other arguments are not acceptable explanations for outright centralized control of the content of news and information. Some poor countries allow for the exchange of diverse views, while some developed countries restrict content diversity. We seek to recognize press freedom wherever it exists, in poor and rich countries, as well as in countries of various ethnic, religious, and cultural backgrounds.

This survey does not assess the degree to which the press in any country serves responsibly, reflecting a high ethical standard. The issue of "press responsibility" is often raised to defend governmental control of the press. Indeed, a truly irresponsible press does a disservice to its public and diminishes its own credibility. However, governmental efforts to rein in the press on the pretext of making the press "responsible" has far worse results, in most cases. This issue is reflected in the degree of freedom in the flow of information as assessed in the survey.

Sources

Our data come from correspondents overseas, staff travel, international visitors, the findings of human rights and press freedom organizations, specialists in geographic and geopolitical areas, the reports of governments and multilateral bodies, and a variety of domestic and international news media. We would particularly like to thank other members of the International Freedom of Expression eXchange (IFEX) network for providing detailed and timely analyses of press freedom violations in a variety of countries worldwide.

Methodology

Through the years, we have refined and expanded our methodology. Recent changes to our methodology are intended to simplify the presentation of information without altering the comparability of data for a given country over the 24-year span of the Survey's existence, or of the comparative ratings of all countries over that period.

Our examination of the level of press freedom in each country is divided into three broad categories: the legal environment, political influences, and economic pressures.

▌ The **legal environment** encompasses an examination of the laws and regulations that could influence media content as well as the government's inclination to use these laws to restrict the ability of media to operate. We assess the positive impact of legal and constitutional guarantees for freedom of expression, as well as the potentially negative aspects of security legislation, the penal code and other criminal statutes, penalties for libel and defamation, and registration requirements for both media outlets and journalists.

▌ In considering **political influences,** we evaluate the degree of political control over the content of news media. Issues examined in this category include access to information and sources, editorial independence, official censorship and self-censorship, the ability of the media to operate freely and without harassment, and the intimidation of journalists by the state or other actors.

▌ Finally, we examine **economic pressures** on the media, which include the structure of media ownership, the costs of establishing media outlets as well as of production and distribution, the selective withholding of state advertising or subsidies, official bias in licensing, and the impact of corruption and bribery on content.

Ratings

Each country is rated in these three categories, with the higher numbers indicating less freedom. A country's total score is based on the total of the three categories: a score of 0–30 places the country in the Free press group; 31–60 in the Partly Free; and 61–100 in the Not Free press group.

Legend

Country	LEGAL ENVIRONMENT: 0–30 POINTS
	POLITICAL INFLUENCES: 0–40 POINTS
	ECONOMIC PRESSURES: 0–30 POINTS
Status: Free (0–30)	TOTAL SCORE: 0–100 POINTS
Partly Free (31–60)	
Not Free (61–100)	

Press Freedom in 2002

Karin Deutsch Karlekar

Press freedom came under increasing pressure and suffered a notable decline in 2002. Journalists' ability to report freely was hindered by ongoing political conflict and insurgencies, as well as by heightened government-directed restrictions on media outlets. While a number of authoritarian regimes continued to stifle independent media, a particularly worrying trend during the year was that in many cases, intimidation and harassment of the press was perpetrated or condoned by nominally democratic governments.

The annual Freedom House survey of press freedom provides a numerical rating for each country as well as categorizing the level of press freedom in each country as "Free," "Partly Free," or "Not Free." Ratings are determined on the basis of an examination of three broad categories: the legal environment in which media operate, political influences on reporting and access to information, and economic pressures on content and the dissemination of news.

In 2002, fully 78 countries (41 percent) out of 193 surveyed were rated Free, while 47 (24 percent) were rated Partly Free and 68 (35 percent) were rated Not Free. The year saw a marked deterioration in press freedom worldwide, as measured by a shift in category. Overall, 4 countries (Dominican Republic, Panama, Peru, and Thailand) declined from Free to Partly Free, while 7 countries (Armenia, Colombia, Jordan, Nepal, Russia, Ukraine, and Venezuela) declined from Partly Free to Not Free. Only 2 countries registered a positive category shift in 2002—Fiji moved

Karin Deutsch Karlekar, a senior researcher at Freedom House, served as managing editor of Freedom of the Press 2003. *She holds a Ph.D. in history from Cambridge University.*

up from Partly Free to Free, and Sri Lanka improved from Not Free to Partly Free.

In terms of population, 20 percent of the world's population lives in countries that enjoy a Free press, while 38 percent have a Partly Free press and 42 percent have a Not Free press. This situation represents a significant decline during the course of the past year, as the proportion of the world's population in the Not Free category increased by four percentage points from last year.

Smaller numerical declines were registered in a number of other states where media outlets and journalists were subjected to a wide range of legal, political, and economic pressures. Other key trends noted in 2002 include:

▮ Marked declines in the Americas and Eurasia

▮ The heightened threat to press freedom posed by political conflict and armed insurgencies

▮ An increased use of politically motivated lawsuits and other criminal charges to harass the media

▮ The threat to diversity of media ownership posed by state takeovers or consolidation of private ownership

▮ A decline in press freedom in a number of electoral democracies

This year's findings demonstrate that the media remain vulnerable, even in many of the world's nominally democratic countries. These governments' use of a wide variety of methods to intimidate the press continues to hinder the ability of journalists to provide independent scrutiny and commentary, which is critically important if governments are to remain accountable.

Regional Trends

Although declines were seen worldwide, negative trends were particularly apparent in the Americas and in Eurasia. In the Americas, 18 countries (52 percent) were rated Free, 13 (37 percent) were rated Partly Free, and 4 (11 percent) were rated Not Free. Colombia and Venezuela joined the ranks of Cuba and Haiti in having the worst environment for the press in the region. Elsewhere in Latin America, scores declined as a result of economic pressure, continued legal harassment, and the unwillingness of elected governments to tolerate scrutiny from independent media outlets. The regional economic downturn negatively affected the press in a number of countries, most notably in Argentina, Bolivia, Guatemala, and Honduras. Meanwhile, the use of the courts as a method of censoring journalists was on the rise in Brazil and Uruguay.

Although just over half the countries in the region have media that are classified as Free, a number of formerly Free countries slipped into the Partly Free category during 2002. In the Dominican Republic, the concentration of media ownership, coupled with the government's selective placement of advertisements, imposed a growing financial burden on the independent press. Panama's rating fell as a result of the sustained and widespread legal campaign against critical journalists by public officials; as a result of that campaign, more than 90 journalists are facing criminal libel or defamation charges. Peru, which had been rated Free in 2001, slipped back into the Partly Free category as people associated with the Toledo administration brought legal charges against the media for libel or for reporting on corruption. Journalists faced threats and assaults as well. The backsliding during 2002 by this new, democratically elected government underscores the reality that in fledgling democracies, the media often continue to face considerable pressures as a result of restrictive legislation or a politicized judiciary.

In Central Europe and Eurasia, declines also outweighed gains in 2002. In this year's survey, 9 countries (33 percent) were classified as Free, 8 (30 percent) as Partly Free, and 10 (37 percent) as Not Free. The percentage of countries with Not Free media increased dramatically as three countries slipped from Partly Free to Not Free in 2002. While declines in the Americas can be attributed to a number of reasons, the overriding concern in countries of the former Soviet Union is the pressure placed on independent media outlets by the state. In Macedonia, several independent broadcasters were forcibly closed for the duration of the parliamentary election campaign, while state-run media displayed a marked bias in favor of the ruling party. Authorities also threatened and charged journalists with criminal libel if they "disgraced" the government during the campaign period. Meanwhile, officials in Kazakhstan cracked down on investigative reporters, charging several with alleged offenses in response to their coverage of corruption and human rights issues.

State harassment was the primary factor in downgrading Armenia, Russia, and Ukraine from Partly Free to Not Free in 2002. In both Russia and Armenia, the public's access to diverse sources of information was curtailed by the closing of leading independent television broadcasters. In addition, Armenian authorities repeatedly used security legislation and criminal libel laws to stifle critical coverage, while Russian and Ukrainian journalists are frequently targeted by politically motivated libel lawsuits, criminal charges, safety inspections, and obstructive tax audits. Reporters in all three countries, particularly those who investigate alleged official corruption or present critical views, continue to be subjected to intimidation and violent attacks, including murder. Furthermore, credible investigations into these crimes are rarely undertaken. (A number of additional constraints facing media outlets in Russia and Ukraine are explored in the essay by Thomas A. Dine on page 41 of this volume.) However, one of the most worrying aspects of this regional decline is that state-directed intimidation of the media and attempts to influence media outlets are being perpetrated by democratically elected governments that seem to be increasingly fearful of critical coverage.

The overall level of press freedom remained largely unchanged in Europe, Asia, Africa, and the Middle East, despite gains or declines in a number of individual countries. Western Europe continued to boast the highest level of press freedom worldwide, with 24 countries (96 percent) rated Free and 1 (4 percent) rated Partly Free. The Asia Pacific region also exhibited a relatively high level of press freedom, with 18 countries (46 percent) rated Free, 7 (18 percent) rated Partly Free, and 14 (36 percent) rated Not Free. Improvements were balanced by declines in 2002, as Fiji and Sri Lanka moved up in category while Thailand and Nepal were downgraded. In contrast, no category changes took place in Sub-Saharan Africa, where 8 countries (17 percent) were rated Free, 16 (33 percent) were rated Partly Free, and 24 (50 percent) were rated Not Free. The region with the worst conditions for the media in 2002 continued to be the Middle East and North Africa, with 1 country (5 percent) rated Free, 2 (11 percent) rated Partly Free, and 16 (84 percent) rated Not Free.

Positive Trends during the Year

Despite an overall global decline in the level of press freedom, certain countries did register positive change during 2002. The biggest numerical shift of the year was seen in Sri Lanka, whose rating improved from Not

Free to Partly Free. A lasting bilateral ceasefire agreement between the government and Liberation Tigers of Tamil Eelam rebels signed in February, accompanied by continuing peace talks, led to a more open environment for the media throughout the year, particularly regarding the limits of permissible coverage and access to areas previously under rebel control. In addition, newly elected Prime Minister Ranil Wickremasinghe demonstrated a commitment to removing legal restrictions on the media, and in June, the Sri Lankan parliament voted to repeal the criminal defamation law.

Greater political stability also led to an improved press freedom rating for Fiji, which joined a number of its Pacific neighbors in being rated Free. Under the Qarase administration elected in August 2001, overt harassment of the media has declined and journalists are generally able to report freely on controversial issues. An end to civil wars in Angola and Chad led to somewhat greater space for the media to operate, while progress was also noted in the post-conflict states of Somalia and Afghanistan as a result of the growth in the number of independent media outlets. Elsewhere in the world, the passage of reformist media legislation in 2002 contributed to noticeable improvements in Bosnia, Yugoslavia (Serbia and Montenegro), Azerbaijan, and Bahrain.

Conflict and Insurgency Take a Toll

In a number of countries, press freedom has been progressively compromised by political instability or civil conflict. The ability of the media to operate freely and impartially can become especially hampered when media outlets are seen to be providing overt editorial support to a particular side in the conflict. Three countries—Colombia, Nepal, and Venezuela—entered the ranks of the Not Free countries during 2002 as a result of such pressures.

An intensification of the Maoist insurgency in Nepal, coupled with more aggressive tactics employed by the government to fight it, had a negative impact on Nepal's press environment in 2002. After declaring a state of emergency in November 2001, which broadened restrictions on permissible coverage, authorities arrested more than 100 journalists during 2002 under the provisions of a new antiterrorism ordinance. Although the majority had no connection to the Maoist rebels and were held for short periods of time, more than a dozen remain incarcerated. Reporters have also been threatened and violently attacked by the Maoists. In Colombia, right-wing paramilitaries and Marxist guerillas in a continuing armed conflict routinely target both local and foreign journalists. A number of murders during the year, repeated harassment and threats against reporters, and economic pressures on media outlets combined to cause a further decline in Colombia's level of press freedom. Meanwhile, a dramatic deterioration in political stability in neighboring Venezuela in 2002 led to the largest numerical decline of the year as well as to a category downgrade. However, in this case the media were not merely caught between opposing factions in an increasingly polarized atmosphere; instead, media outlets took an active role in opposing the government of President Hugo Chavez. Responding to Chavez's verbal antagonism towards the media, as well as harassment and physical attacks on journalists by his supporters, many private media outlets adopted a pronounced anti-Chavez slant, and coverage became decidedly biased during the course of the year.

In all three countries, political or military strife, coupled with the targeting of the media by some or all parties to the conflict, led to significant declines in the level of press freedom by encouraging fear and self-censorship, and by creating a climate of impunity in which those who infringe on the media's rights are not punished for their actions. Political tension in the wake of a disputed December 2001 presidential election, which threatened to destabilize Madagascar during the first several months of 2002, also had a negative impact on the ability of the local media to report impartially on the crisis, as journalists and media outlets with connections to both factions became the targets of attack. However, a legal resolution to the dispute in April restored a measure of stability to the island nation. Media independence was similarly compromised by a protracted political crisis triggered by a rebel insurgency that erupted in Cote d'Ivoire in September. While authorities jammed the signals of foreign media outlets, local journalists and newspapers suspected of antigovernment bias were subjected to harassment and attacks. Elsewhere, ongoing armed conflicts in Liberia and in the Israeli-administered Territories/Palestinian Authority led to a further decline in the numerical scores for these two entities.

Continuing Government-Directed Pressure on the Media

A more worrying trend in 2002, already noted in the case of several countries in the former Soviet Union but also apparent worldwide, is the imposition of additional restrictions on the press by the state. These attempts to silence or intimidate independent media outlets take a variety of forms—restrictive laws and politically motivated prosecutions, censorship, verbal and physical harassment, careful direction of advertising revenue—and have long been used by repressive regimes to strengthen their control over critical voices. However, the use of these tactics, which have become increasingly sophisticated, has spread to elected governments in fragile democracies that are equally wary of criticism and scrutiny.

Flagrant state repression against journalists and media outlets continued to be a problem in certain countries throughout the year. The five worst-rated countries in 2002 were Burma, Cuba, Iraq, North Korea, and Turkmenistan. In these states, independent media are either nonexistent or barely able to operate, and the role of the press is to act as a mouthpiece for the ruling regime. Other authoritarian governments also extended their control over the media through a variety of means. In Zimbabwe, the Mugabe administration passed draconian legislation that further restricted the ability of both foreign and local reporters to work freely. Eritrea's dramatic 2001 crackdown against the independent media, ostensibly on the grounds of national security, continued; all private newspapers have been banned and 18 journalists remain in prison. In Togo, an amendment to the press code that increased the penalties for defamation was used to arrest a number of journalists, and official pressure on advertisers has endangered the financial viability of many independent publications. Haitian authorities continue to disregard legal provisions for press freedom and impede investigations into the murders of two journalists, and the press faced increased harassment and violence at the hands of government supporters throughout the year.

In a number of countries, regimes focused on controlling content on the Internet as a way of suppressing independent voices. Tunisian authorities aggressively monitor Web sites, and in June the founder of a satirical Internet site was sentenced to two years in prison for spreading "false information." In the Maldives, four Internet writers were tried for defamation and three were sentenced to life imprisonment. The governments of China and Vietnam continue to block access to politically sensitive Web sites and to arrest and imprison cyber-dissidents.

State directed intimidation was not confined to authoritarian regimes, however. Jordan's crackdown against the press, begun in late 2001, continued in 2002 with the adoption of additional legal regulations under which journalists were prosecuted for criticizing the government or for publishing "false information." In addition, the government closed the local bureau of Al-Jazeera after the Qatar-based satellite news channel aired a program in which participants criticized Jordanian foreign policy.

The impact of sustained pressure on the media meant that Jordan was downgraded from Partly Free to Not Free in 2002. The situation for Bangladesh's independent press also continued to deteriorate during the course of the year. In a polarized political environment, journalists continue to be targeted by members of political parties, criminals, and Islamic fundamentalists as a result of their investigations into corruption and human rights issues. In addition, the government has become increasingly sensitive to the reports of foreign media organizations. In December, a number of foreign and local journalists were arrested, detained by security forces, and tortured while in custody after they attempted to report on the rise of Islamic fundamentalism in the country.

That fledgling democracies seem increasingly intolerant of scrutiny and ever more willing to restrict the ability of the media to report freely was highlighted this year in the case of Thailand, which was downgraded from Free to Partly Free in 2002. The heightened sensitivity to criticism on the part of Thaksin Shinawatra's administration became apparent early in the year, when editions of two international publications were banned and the government threatened to deport two foreign journalists. Meanwhile, local media groups faced increased official pressure to tone down critical reporting, programming was taken off the air, and several editors were forced to resign. As Thaksin consolidates his party's hold over bureaucratic structures and increases the power of the executive, he seems unwilling to allow the press, as well as other independent institutions designed to check corruption, to continue in their role as independent watchdogs of the government.

Conclusions

Increased state-directed pressure on the media and the global decline in press freedom noted in this year's survey come at a time when overall democracy trends are holding steady. Indeed, this year's edition of *Freedom in the World*, Freedom House's annual survey of political rights and civil liberties, noted that gains for freedom were made in a number of countries during 2002 and that improvements in score outweighed declines by a three-to-one ratio. However, a comparison on both surveys reveals that 35 countries are rated in a lower category on press freedom than they are in terms of their general political and civil freedoms.

How does one explain this discrepancy? One possible explanation is that although 121 of the world's 192 governments can be considered electoral democracies, the presence of a minimum standard of electoral conduct does not automatically lead to other attributes of a mature democracy, such as strong civic institutions, an independent judiciary, and vibrant and free media. In relatively new or fragile democracies, the press is often considered to be a nuisance that must be managed or exploited, rather than as an independent watchdog that should be allowed to freely scrutinize official policies and practice. The rising level of violations of press freedom by democratically elected regimes, often by varied and subtle means, is a reminder that in many societies, progress in political rights has not yet been matched by commensurate advances in civil liberties. This trend poses a serious challenge to a deepening of freedom and democracy around the world, and must continue to be carefully monitored.

Free / 0 to 10

Andorra
Belgium
Finland
Iceland
Marshall Islands
Monaco
New Zealand
Norway
Palau
Saint Lucia
San Marino
Sweden
Switzerland

Free / 11 to 20

Australia
Bahamas
Barbados
Canada
Costa Rica
Cyprus
Denmark
Dominica
Estonia
France
Germany
Grenada
Ireland
Jamaica
Japan
Latvia
Liechtenstein
Lithuania
Luxembourg
Malta
Micronesia
Netherlands

Poland
Portugal
Saint Kitts and Nevis
Saint Vincent and
   the Grenadines
Sao Tome and
   Principe
Slovenia
Spain
Tuvalu
United Kingdom
United States

Free / 21 to 30

Austria
Belize
Benin
Bolivia
Botswana
Bulgaria
Cape Verde
Chile
Czech Republic
East Timor
Fiji
Ghana
Greece
Guyana
Hungary
Israel
Italy
Kiribati
Korea, South
Mali
Mauritius
Nauru
Papua New Guinea

Philippines
Samoa
Slovakia
Solomon Islands
South Africa
Suriname
Taiwan
Trinidad and Tobago
Uruguay
Vanuatu

Partly Free / 31 to 40

Argentina
Brazil
Burkina Faso
Croatia
Dominican Republic
El Salvador
Madagascar
Mexico
Mongolia
Namibia
Nicaragua
Panama
Peru
Romania
Senegal
Thailand
Tonga
Yugoslavia

Partly Free / 41 to 50

Albania
Antigua and Barbuda
Bosnia
Comoros
Ecuador

India
Lesotho
Macedonia
Mozambique
Seychelles
Tanzania
Uganda

Partly Free / 51 to 60
Congo-Brazzaville
Gabon
Georgia
Guatemala
Guinea-Bissau
Honduras
Indonesia
Kuwait
Malawi
Moldova
Morocco
Niger
Nigeria
Pakistan
Paraguay
Sri Lanka
Turkey

Not Free / 61 to 70
Algeria
Armenia
Bahrain
Bangladesh
Bhutan
Cambodia
Cameroon
Central African
 Republic

Chad
Colombia
Cote d'Ivoire
Djibouti
Ethiopia
The Gambia
Jordan
Kenya
Maldives
Mauritania
Nepal
Qatar
Russia
Sierra Leone
Singapore
Ukraine
Venezuela
Yemen
Zambia

Not Free / 71 to 80
Afghanistan
Angola
Azerbaijan
Brunei
Burundi
China
Egypt
Guinea
Haiti
Iran
Kazakhstan
Kyrgyzstan
Laos
Lebanon
Liberia
Malaysia

Oman
Rwanda
Saudi Arabia
Somalia
Swaziland
Syria
Tajikistan
Togo
Tunisia
United Arab Emirates

Not Free / 81 to 90
Belarus
Congo-Kinshasa
Equatorial Guinea
Eritrea
Israeli-Administered
 Territories/
 Palestinian
 Authority
Libya
Sudan
Uzbekistan
Vietnam
Zimbabwe

Not Free / 91 to 100
Burma
Cuba
Iraq
Korea, North
Turkmenistan

Summary of Results

Regional Press Freedom Breakdown

Region	Free	Partly Free	Not Free	Number of Countries
Americas	18	13	4	35
Asia Pacific	18	7	14	39
CEE-FSU	9	8	10	27
Middle East & North Africa	1	2	16	19
Sub-Saharan Africa	8	16	24	48
Western Europe	24	1	0	25
Total	**78**	**47**	**68**	**193**

Press Freedom by Population

Status	By Country	By Population (millions)
Free	78 (41%)	1,235 (20%)
Partly Free	47 (24%)	2,332 (38%)
Not Free	68 (35%)	2,634 (42%)
Total	**193 (100%)**	**6,201 (100%)**

Press Freedom,
the Past Quarter Century:
The Vile and the Valiant

Leonard R. Sussman

The past quarter century has been marked by steady gains for press freedom in all parts of the world. To be sure, it has also featured the murder of nearly a thousand journalists, the imprisonment of thousands more, and efforts to censor the press by methods both crude and subtle. However, despite backsliding and occasional setbacks, the general momentum has been towards greater freedom, less censorship, and expanded influence for independent media around the world.

The expansion of press freedom has accompanied an overall spread of freedom and democracy that has affected every part of the world. To a substantial degree, the reasons behind the growth of press freedom are much the same as the reasons behind the wave of political freedom that has swept the former Communist countries and much of what was once called the Third World. In the case of press freedom, however, there is an additional element: the central role played by the modern press freedom movement.

The origins of the press freedom movement can be traced to what is known as the UNESCO censorship wars. This year, 2003, is a milestone because America is rejoining the UN Educational, Scientific, and Cultural Organization (UNESCO) after 19 years on the sidelines. Today's

Leonard R. Sussman is a senior scholar in international communications at Freedom House. His books include: Press Freedom in Our Genes: A Human Need *(2001),* Democracy's Advocate: A History of Freedom House *(2002), and* A Passion for Freedom: My Encounters with Extraordinary People *(forthcoming).*

UNESCO is far different from the organization of 1976, when it called for a New World Information and Communication Order (NWICO)—a global project to pressure news media worldwide to carry the "good news" emanating from developing countries, a campaign that was widely interpreted in the West as an international sanction for censorship.

The First Global Assault

UNESCO's 1976 conference on news flows was the first global confrontation between the state and the journalism community. What made the confrontation significant was that the forces of censorship seemed to have an ally in the large, influential, and respected institution of the United Nations. In the days of the League of Nations, before World War II, there had been acrimonious international conferences on censorship and related matters. These debates, however, took place behind closed doors and produced only verbose resolutions that few respected.

The UNESCO controversy was different. It was, to begin with, initiated by more than 100 developing countries, who were organized under the rubric of the Nonaligned Movement. The "nonaligned" call for NWICO was soon endorsed by the Soviet Union and its satellites. NWICO, despite some valid critiques of Western journalism, became yet another weapon in the Cold War debate. Some proposed cures for "unbalanced" international reporting were little more than transparent justifications for censorship. These included the licensing of journalists and the penalizing of violators of a government-produced code of press "ethics" and coverage. Although UNESCO did not subscribe to all such measures, it did provide a forum where such propositions for enhanced state control of the press could be aired and taken seriously.

UNESCO and the Nonaligned Movement attempted to make governmental regulation of the press the acceptable global norm. For decades, censorship schemes had been advanced at scores of international political, academic, and journalistic conferences. Third World government spokesmen repeatedly challenged the West's "free flow of information" concept. Seldom invited to the debates were journalists from these countries. They were the chief victims of "development journalism," a concept defined by its defenders as mobilizing the mass media for the purpose of stimulating economic growth. Clearly, the governments pushing hardest for NWICO were the same governments that already owned, controlled, or strongly influenced most aspects of the print and broadcast news media in their own countries.

The Soviet draft before UNESCO's 1976 conference summed up the NWICO case in one sentence: "[S]tates are responsible for the activities in the international sphere of all mass media under their jurisdiction." UNESCO would also attempt to define the legal "right to communicate," including "the right of reply through the communication media at the international level." In other words, at the request of a foreign government, Washington officials would be compelled to instruct a private news service such as the Associated Press what to carry on its wires.

The issue was joined: Must development journalism hamper or replace freedom of the press? Proponents of broad government control of mass communications—in addition to their efforts to link news agencies to economic development—claimed that Western news agencies distorted or ignored Third World news while transmitting information mainly of interest to the industrialized West. This was called "cultural imperialism."

There was, clearly, a substantial constituency for such arguments. In 1976, *Freedom in the World*, the Freedom House survey of political rights and civil liberties, showed only 39 of 159 nations rated "Free" on the civil liberties scale, which included freedom of the press as a criterion.

The campaign against press freedom continued in 1977, even as global concern for human rights expanded—pushed by new U.S. president Jimmy Carter. The secretariat of UNESCO, in combination with a group of Marxist academics, generated what was called "the progressive radicalization of the UNESCO position." There was a major battle over the wording of a Soviet-inspired text on the press. A number of organizations, including Freedom House, participated in a redrafting of the statement. The UNESCO staff, however, repeatedly restored the text's objectionable language.

In response to the mounting criticism, Western media representatives explained that their limited coverage of developing countries was in part due to the expense of assigning reporters on a permanent basis to countries that seldom generated news that would interest a global audience. Local journalists, they added, often lacked credibility because their reporting was influenced by the dictates of oppressive regimes.

Press Defense Begins

Prior to UNESCO's having taken up the news-flow question, American media seldom carried stories about the murder or oppression of developing world journalists. Only after the international press-control campaign began did American news media publicize the connection between oppression of journalism in Third World countries and the future of press freedom worldwide. Eventually, a connection was drawn between the movement for global censorship and the freedoms enjoyed by Western journalists. It was at this point that the modern movement for press freedom was formed.

A coordinated defense of press freedom got underway in mid-1976, when Freedom House issued an alert that got the attention of the press and policy makers in the United States. The World Press Freedom Committee (WPFC), under the leadership of George Beebe, then associate publisher of the *Miami Herald*, began answering the drumbeat of attacks on the free press. The counterattack, however, developed slowly.

Then Freedom House began reporting direct violations of press freedom, little attention was paid to this rapidly growing phenomenon. The significant progress in placing press freedom on the international agenda is attributable to a small group of activist organizations (see box).

International Freedom of Expression eXchange (1992)More than 50 associations on every continent have been linked over the Internet since 1992 by the International Freedom of Expression eXchange (IFEX). Its members carry immediate news of press freedom violations to some 2,000 subscribers worldwide. They, in turn, protest directly to offending nations

Press Freedom Advocates

International Association of the Periodical Press (founded 1925)

Freedom House (1941)

Inter American Press Association (1942)

International Association of Broadcasting (1946)

World Association of Newspapers (1948)

International Press Institute (1950)

Commonwealth Press Union (1950)

International Federation of Journalists (1952)

World Press Freedom Committee (1976)

Committee to Protect Journalists (1981)

Reporters Sans Frontieres (1985)

and may visit countries to discuss offenses. In a recent year, IFEX recorded several thousand press freedom violations. The organization has also provided resources to such developing groups as the Media Institute of Southern Africa (MISA). In several regions, leading journalists also worked ceaselessly to spotlight massive violations of press freedom.

In 1978, after six years of bitter debate, UNESCO finally approved the Mass Media Declaration. The declaration was considerably watered down from previous versions. It actually lent support to a free press, omitted earlier references to press controls, and implicitly promised to improve Western reporting of developing countries and bolster their communication capabilities. The text called for "a wider and better balanced dissemination of information." Third World and Marxist hard-liners would continue, nevertheless, to demand a form of NWICO.

A two-year consultation by 16 representatives of Eastern, Western, and Third World communication specialists concluded in 1979. This initiative, part of the 1976 compromise at Nairobi to prevent the breakup of UNESCO, was less antagonistic to the free press than had been anticipated. The book-length MacBride report agreed that there was no single model for journalism in a world that is pluralistic. The final report condemned all censorship and said journalists must have access to a variety of private and public views. Licensing of journalists was rejected. No support was given for the creation of a universal code of ethics, and there was no special reference to the need for the "protection of journalists," a code term for governmental licensing of the press.

As the UNESCO press-control campaign lost some of its steam, however, the debate entered the UN General Assembly through its Committee on Information. There, for years to come, NWICO would be promoted by the same alliance of Soviet and Third World players, with the same arguments made familiar at UNESCO. Only after UNESCO defanged NWICO in 1983 did the United Nations decide not to push the issue further.

Survey of Press Freedom

By 1979 it had become clear that a continuing examination of press freedom worldwide was needed. Freedom House thus launched the first annual *Survey of Press Freedom*. This survey would provide universal criteria by which to assess separately the print and broadcast media in every country. The survey examined each nation's press laws and their administration, the political and economic influences on the content of news reporting, and any violations of press freedom—murders, harassment, and arrests of journalists, as well as the banning of publications or broadcasts. The freedom of foreign journalists within each nation would also be assessed.

The first survey, published in 1980, made one highly significant finding. A half century earlier there had been 39 national news agencies in 28 countries. Seventy percent of these were nominally independent of the government. As a consequence of the UNESCO challenges to the news media in the 1970s, the number of government-operated news agencies increased rapidly. In 1980, fully 68 percent of countries had government-operated news agencies, many of which controlled news entering the country as well as domestic news coverage. Of the nations with the lowest civil liberties rating as measured by Freedom House, 95 percent operated government news agencies.

Meanwhile, press regulation or control continued to be widely debated among academics. An acknowledged leader of this debate was Kaarle Nordenstreng, chairman of the Department of Journalism at the University of Tampere, Finland, and president of the International Organization of Journalists (IOJ). The IOJ, funded from Moscow, had split off from the International Press Institute at the outset of the Cold War. Nordenstreng argued that the UNESCO debates over "national sovereignty" for the news media of developing countries "may be understood best as a step in the still larger struggle to break the domination of the world business system."

The significance of this argument would surface more than 20 years later as the world prepared for two World Summits on the Information Society (WSIS) in 2003 and 2005. Having lost the immediate NWICO objectives, many of the same players are pressing for regulation of the content flows on the Internet. (See Ronald Koven's essay, page 31.)

As the 1980s began, UNESCO's program-setting conference created a problem for Western delegates, who wanted to help improve Third World communications without accepting press control as part of a development package. As the ideological debates continued, free-press advocates would acknowledge that Third World demands for expanded communication facilities were valid and, indeed, necessary for democratic governance. At international media conferences, however, the continuing cacophony sounded to independent journalists as though all groups—thoroughly oppressive regimes, moderate developing countries, and the Marxist bloc—wanted governmental control of worldwide journalism. Moderate developing countries that simply wanted better news coverage were thus linked to a Leninist definition of journalism in these debates.

The Declaration of Talloires and the End of NWICO

The first coordinated counterattack by the free press was mounted in 1981 by the World Press Freedom Committee (WPFC) at Talloires, a small town in the French Alps. Ninety media leaders from 25 countries, developing and developed alike, produced the Declaration of Talloires. The declaration vowed to "improve the free flow of information worldwide and resist any encroachment on this free flow." In a pluralistic world, said the declaration, there can be no international code of journalistic ethics; journalists must have access to diverse sources of news and information, official and unofficial, without restriction. It added: "We oppose any proposals that would control journalists in the name of protecting them"—a reference to licensing journalists under the guise of protecting them on dangerous assignments.

The declaration concluded: "Press freedom is a basic human right. We pledge ourselves to concerted action to uphold this fight." The Declaration of Talloires became a fundamental document in the history of the press freedom struggle.

In addition to providing a marker for press freedom advocates and critics, the Declaration of Talloires galvanized the U.S. Congress to action. A House of Representatives resolution warned UNESCO that if it set back press freedom, America would withdraw its financial support from the organization. UNESCO never did move to license or otherwise inhibit journalists, but it continued to provide a forum for those who wanted to do so.

UNESCO's director-general, Amadou Mahtar M'Bow, told an interviewer in 1981 that he would act always in support of democracy and press freedom. He stated privately, however, that as an international civil servant he must operate within his mandate; that is to say, he must adhere to the wishes of the governments that were involved in UNESCO debates. In fact, M'Bow went a step further by advancing proposals for press-control programs that a majority of governments, mainly from the Third World, greeted with approval.

The licensing of journalists was such an issue. Thirteen countries in Latin America already licensed reporters. To license implies the power to revoke a license when the state objects to a reporter's work. A long campaign to end press licensing in Latin America reached the Inter-American Commission on Human Rights in 1984. The commission, however, voted 5 to 1 to support Costa Rica's press-licensing law. The sole dissenter was the deputy executive director of Freedom House, the only North American on the commission.

The issue next moved to the Inter-American Court of Human Rights. The court concluded unanimously that "the compulsory licensing of journalists is incompatible with … the American Convention on Human Rights insofar as it denies some persons access to the full use of the news media as a means of expressing themselves or imparting information." The court's ruling also encompassed the right of readers, viewers, and listeners as well. Several years later, the government of Costa Rica ended the licensing of journalists.

In 1983, UNESCO approved the resolution, initially set forth by Freedom House, which pledged that the organization would never impose an "information order" on the world media. Other budgetary and administrative changes urged by the United States were also approved. Nevertheless, the Reagan administration announced that the United States would withdraw from UNESCO in January 1985. At that time, I was vice chairman of the U.S. National Commission for UNESCO (created by the State Department). We at the commission opposed the withdrawal and urged that the United States remain in UNESCO to fight for further changes. However, the United States pulled out of the organization. It was followed by the United Kingdom a year later.

In 1988, Director-General M'Bow was defeated in an election for the top post by Federico Mayor. A series of institutional reforms followed. Most striking was Mayor's commitment to a free press. He said that NWICO was now "history."

Mayor also arranged the first regional press freedom conference at Windhoek, Namibia, in 1991. Independent African journalists met with government officials to produce the Windhoek Declaration. It called for steps to enhance press freedom on a continent where the oppression of journalists was widespread. The declaration was adopted the following year in Kazakhstan at a similar press freedom meeting for Central Asia. Other UNESCO press freedom conferences were held in Latin America and the Middle East. Improvements, however, came slowly. Mayor also designated May 3 as the annual World Press Freedom Day, dedicated to a celebration of journalistic liberty and the assessment of threats to press freedom. In addition, the director-general personally issued protests to various governments that were violating journalistic freedoms in their countries.

Pressures from the CSCE

The next major development in press freedom was the introduction of glasnost in the Soviet Union by its new leader, Mikhail Gorbachev. Glasnost was an integral part of Gorbachev's strategy to resuscitate the moribund Soviet economy and enable his country to more effectively compete with the West. Gorbachev ended prior censorship of publications, broadcasts, and films. Editorial choice became the responsibility of the editors, most of whom were party members. Gorbachev's purpose was to encourage more creative use of new communication technologies to further *perestroika*, or the development of the economy. Whatever Gorbachev's intentions, glasnost clearly contributed to the implosion of the Soviet empire in 1991.

Another factor in the Soviet breakup was the 15-year exposure of the Soviet bureaucracy to ideological challenges from free societies within the Commission on Security and Cooperation in Europe (CSCE). The CSCE should be credited with prying open some doors for diverse, if not fully free, journalism in Russia.

The CSCE, created in 1975, addressed many issues in three categories: security, economics, and human rights. The Soviet Union welcomed the CSCE as a means of legitimizing the division of Europe after World War II. The Soviets accepted the inclusion of human rights issues without realizing that they would become the Achilles' heel of the entrenched Communist bureaucracies in Eastern and Central Europe, as well as in Moscow. The CSCE's Final Act called for repeated international conferences to examine progress made in the three categories. The chairman of Freedom House, Max M. Kampelman, served for three years as the American ambassador at CSCE's Madrid conference. The conference featured frequent clashes over human rights violations, mainly those attributed to the Soviet bloc. Kampelman named victims, asked pertinent questions, and forced the Communist bureaucracies to respond in the public arena.

The demise of the Soviet Union in 1991 generated immediate changes in press freedom throughout Eastern Europe. For the first time, Russian news media enjoyed a modest degree of freedom. There were, however, problems as new media outlets were dominated by oligarchs who used the press to advance the business and political agendas of their vast corporate holdings. Despite the reduction of overt political control, threats to Russian journalists greatly increased. Prominent investigative reporters were killed, beaten, or blatantly threatened. Self-censorship increased. The news media were freer than they had been under Communist rule, but at a toll in physical violence. By the turn of the century, the credibility of the Russian press was significantly diminished.

Laws to Enforce Press "Responsibility"

In the 1990s, the market economy replaced the centralized Communist model across Russia, the Baltic States, and Central and Eastern Europe. The winds of change blew across the countries of Africa as well, prompting the start of a more diverse flow of news and information.

While the surge in democracy ushered in an era of unprecedented press freedom and diversity, it also generated a new set of challenges from governments that found a free and often aggressive media environment to be an obstacle and a nuisance. By 1993, post–Cold War tensions generated widespread proposals in Eastern and Central Europe, the former Soviet Union, and Africa to restrict journalists. Only totalitarian states still defended censorship. Yet there were increasing efforts to enforce rules to guarantee press "responsibility." Even European democracies joined the bandwagon. Sensational reports of domestic political escapades angered officials in Italy, France, Germany, and the United Kingdom. In some former Communist countries, public frustration over unfulfilled promises and mediocre news media fed official efforts to restrict journalists.

Most troubling were proposals by Western European nations through the Council of Europe to consider the adoption of a code of journalistic ethics and a mechanism to regulate press fairness. The Parliamentary Assembly of the council defended the action as encouraging truth and integrity in reporting.

At meetings in Asia and Africa, developing countries signaled a desire to rewrite Article 19 of the Universal Declaration of Human Rights. The article, which defines press freedom, stipulates that no restrictions be placed on the media. Article 19 is a key press freedom document; it is often invoked whenever the rights of journalists are under threat. Now, some developing countries were challenging Western definitions of human rights and singling out press freedom for particular attention. Some Asian rulers, notably Prime Minister Mahathir Mohamad of Malaysia, had long argued that "Asian values" must determine press standards in Asia. As applied to journalism, Asian values entailed consensus building, not adversarial reporting, and a modulated tone to avoid stirring up popular dissent. However, Asian specialist W. T. de Bary has argued that the "Asian values" argument involves the invocation of ancient traditions to preserve and increase a modem government's centralized political authority.

The final document of a Third World human rights conference equivocated on press freedom. It offered the media "freedom and protection"—but only "guaranteed within the framework of national law." That would leave news media hostage to domestic politics without the protection of internationally accepted freedom codes such as Article 19 of the Universal Declaration.

The press freedom controversy would continue for several years within the Council of Europe. In this debate, the phrase "press responsibility" became a code word for restrictions on the news media short of censorship. The Council of Europe debate had important international implications. A five-year study (1992–1996) by the WPFC of the 1950 European Convention on Human Rights revealed that the convention or its equivalents were used nearly 1,200 times in 109 countries to justify the prosecution or jailing of journalists, the closing of independent news media outlets, or other actions meant to stifle press coverage.

Such law-based restrictions were widely examined in the *Survey of Press Freedom 1995* (which appeared in *Freedom in the World 1995*), the bloodiest "pressticidal" year on record—126 journalists were killed in 27 countries; 38 were kidnapped or "disappeared"; another 193 were beaten or otherwise assaulted; and more than 345 were arrested or detained. Governments seemed more interested in "press ethics" than in journalists' safety. Even in many countries with a free press, the press's moral authority was repeatedly challenged, most notably by political debates over press ethics. Draft statutes assigning moral standards for journalism subtly avoided the implicit onus of government pressure, while placing journalists on the defensive for acts labeled libelous or subversive; that is, acts that were not protected by guarantees of press freedom.

As country after country became an electoral democracy, the urge to adopt press-responsibility codes spread widely. In 1994 alone, 16 countries significantly increased statutory controls over the news media. Another 15 less drastically curtailed press freedom. There were, of course, press freedom gains; the news was not all bad. However, these improvements did not offset increased controls. The worsening condition of journalists in 31 countries that year sent a warning that reformist expectations in the post–Cold War era were far from realized.

In a number of countries worldwide, legislators considered limiting the freedom of journalists; press laws were contemplated in 43 countries in 1996 alone. Some 33 different kinds of laws were advanced to threaten, regulate, or even confiscate or ban news media. These laws fell into broad categories: security laws, insult laws, and laws enforcing "responsible journalism."

Security laws would prosecute journalists and/or their employers for threatening national security, "state interests," public order, or even public values. Broadly defined, such potential offenses can target whatever the regime decides it does not like.

Insult laws are more sophisticated. A WPFC study in 2000 reported that in more than 100 countries journalists can be imprisoned for "insulting" government officials and institutions. Such laws, the study concluded, are used to "stifle and punish political discussion and dissent, editorial comment and criticism, satire, and even news that the government would rather hide from the public."

The debate over whether the state should try to enforce responsible journalism led to a paper prepared for the Council of Europe that addressed "the permissible legal limits to the freedom of expression." The paper suggested a modification of the concept of press freedom to protect security, public health, and morals, and oppose racism and violence. In democratic societies, such laws, the paper suggested, would be subject to judicial review. Where the rule of law was fragile, however, such laws could clearly be exploited by ruling elites intent on crushing media criticism.

At the end of the century, however, it could be said that the previous decades had brought remarkable gains for press freedom in nearly every part of the world. A century earlier, there had been no serious movement to expand the reach of a free press to the 95 percent of the world's population that had access only to censored or controlled information, or to no press whatsoever. Three European countries—France, Germany, and the United Kingdom—controlled all the news flowing into or out of Africa, Asia, and much of Latin America. All news from the United States was edited by the European cartel, which was also the carrier of world news to America. Not until the fall of the Berlin Wall in 1989 did areas of the world under Communist domination begin to experience some freedom of the news media.

The Internet—Promise and Problems

The Internet emerged as a major force in mass communications during the last decade of the twentieth century. By 2000, an estimated 400 million persons were using the Internet. Most were in the industrialized countries, but the elites of even the poorest nations were also hooked up to the global system.

In the *Survey of Press Freedom 2001*, Freedom House examined 131 countries for their treatment of the Internet. Countries were judged Most

Restrictive, Moderately Restrictive, or Least Restrictive. We found 59 countries (45 percent) Least Restrictive. This compared with 72 countries (39 percent of the total of 187) regarded as having Free print and broadcast media in the larger survey. The Least Restrictive nations provided liberal access to the Web, and little if any control.

Fifty-three countries had Moderately Restrictive Web policies. Moderate restrictions included political as well as economic limitations on access to the Web and legal or administrative restrictions on content with punishment for violations. This 40 percent related to 28 percent of the countries regarded as having Partly Free print and broadcast media.

Nineteen countries, or 15 percent of the sample, were Most Restrictive. Countries categorized as Most Restrictive may permit only the state-run Internet service provider (ISP) to carry citizens' messages. Even if a private ISP operates, it may be under state surveillance. Citizens are subjected to fines, harassment, imprisonment, or worse for dissenting from official policies or for messages on the Internet deemed seditious. In the survey of print and broadcast media, however, 33 percent of the countries are regarded as being Not Free.

Some optimism for the future was found in this first survey of Web freedom because of the slight variance between the print-and-broadcast rating of some countries and their somewhat more permissive policies with regard to the Internet. This trend was especially notable in several Middle East countries. This glimmer of hope for expanding press freedom in the Middle East, a region long resistant to press freedom, was part of a small but significant series of signs of change in that region. Rulers of Qatar quietly funded Al-Jazeera, the television channel whose frank coverage of Arab and international affairs angered many neighboring regimes. Al-Jazeera also carried lengthy statements by Osama bin Laden, the terrorist leader of al-Qaeda, followed by statements of Secretary of State Colin Powell and other American spokesmen. CNN, unedited, now reached 85 percent of homes in the Persian Gulf region. *Al Sharq Al Awsat*, the Arab newspaper edited in London, circulated in all Arab countries and published opinion columns from the *New York Times*, the *Washington Post*, and the *Christian Science Monitor*.

In 2001, the assault on New York's World Trade Center and the Pentagon led to a series of countermeasures that posed a challenge to press freedom. Defenders of a free press wondered whether press freedom could survive, as unlimited as before, in an environment of enhanced security controls and increased homeland surveillance.

Such questions were openly addressed in democratic countries. New laws enabling the state to monitor electronic communications were enacted; these were opposed by civil libertarians and press freedom advocates. In less democratic nations, the threat of terrorism was quickly exploited to increase pressure on journalists and their institutions. Some authoritarian governments used fear of terrorists to reinforce their illegitimate rule.

In the United States, the Federal Bureau of Investigation (FBI) installed the Carnivore program on private Internet providers such as AOL to enable the government to monitor e-mail messages, trace the trail of communications, and obtain access to stored voice mail. The U.S. attorney general imposed tighter restrictions on the Freedom of Information Act (FOIA), the law that gives journalists and others access to government documents. Other countries—including Australia, Canada, France, Germany, India, and the United Kingdom—took similar measures.

Direct threats by terrorists and preparation for a possible war in Iraq placed America on a limited wartime footing. Louis D. Boccardi, president of the Associated Press, the world's largest news service, said that the challenge for journalists was to "seek a new balance between vigorous advocacy of open government and our understanding as responsible citizens that the nation is now in a fight in which information and openness can be weapons used against us." Adjustments were made, but criticism of such "balancing" was heard as well.

Gains for Press Freedom

Nonetheless, global trends continued in the direction of enhanced press freedom. Ten years after the Windhoek Declaration on Promoting an Independent and Pluralistic African Press, UNESCO convened a representative group of African journalists. While the 1991 session had focused on the print media, the 2001 assembly produced the African Charter on Broadcasting, which called for "promoting respect for freedom of expression, diversity, and the free flow of information and ideas, as well as a three-tier system for broadcasting: public service, commercial, and community." The declaration called for a broadcast media environment that was free of interference, particularly of a political or economic nature. It would still require a dramatic change of policy in most African countries to secure the declaration's goal.

Of great significance is the acceptance of the idea—at long last—that press freedom is an inescapable component of the economic, social, and political development of nations. The linkage was immortalized by Amartya

Sen when he received the 1998 Nobel Prize in Economics. "Press freedom," he stated, is "an integral component of development." The loss of information can have devastating consequences for a society. He attributed the Chinese famine of 1958–1961, in which 23 million to 30 million people died, to "the absence of an uncensored press."

For the future, perhaps the most encouraging factor was the decision by the World Bank to reverse its traditional position on the role of the mass media in economic development. For decades, press freedom advocates had urged the bank to support communication infrastructure in developing countries as a means of gaining diversity in news and information. The bank long refused, arguing that its mandate was to lend money for food, housing, and core development projects.

James D. Wolfensohn, the new president of the World Bank, reversed that policy. He declared that a free press is essential to the economic and political development of poor nations. "The free press is not a luxury," he said; "it is at the core of equitable development." The media, he added, can expose corruption and keep a check on public policy. The press can also enable people to voice diverse opinions on governance and reform and help build public consensus for change. To demonstrate the positive impact of a free press on national development, the bank generated major studies that employed, among others, the Freedom House survey of press freedom.

The policy research working paper (No. 2620) published by the World Bank stated important conclusions under the heading, "Who Owns the Media?": "We found that countries with more prevalent state ownership of the media have less free press, fewer political rights for citizens, inferior governance, less developed markets, and strikingly inferior outcomes in the areas of education and health."

Another hopeful sign is the Declaration of Chapultepec, drafted in 1994 and promoted by the Inter American Press Association. The declaration, signed by 29 countries in the Western Hemisphere, advances 10 principles necessary to guarantee freedom of the press and to support democracy.

A further initiative in Latin America was the 2001 framing of the Lima Principles. The Council of the Peruvian Press, under the direction of Enrique Zileri Gibson and Kela Leon, responded to the challenges presented for a decade by the oppressive presidency of Alberto Fujimori. Rapporteurs from the United Nations and the Organization of American States participated, with 14 other national and foreign specialists. They set forth principles on the right to access and disseminate information, on transparency and development, freedom of journalism and the protection of journalists' sources, limitations on exceptions to the right of access to information, protection of whistleblowers, and legal protection based on the independence of the judiciary. The text concluded: "Any existing regulations which contravene these principles should be abolished."

These and other efforts over many years had an impact on governmental resistance to a free press. For example, Mexico's legislature passed the nation's first freedom-of-information law in 2000. As with every aspect of a democratic society, however, fundamental gains are never assured for eternity but must be reassured through continuing vigilance.

The globalization of news media is a case in point. The amalgamation of large enterprises—newspapers, magazines, radio, television, films, music—into still larger enterprises brought more products to more people worldwide. The diversity of news and views could be limited, however, by "synergy"—the exploitation of one corporate product for delivery by another outlet controlled by the same management. The outcome could be the loss of content variety.

Benjamin Compaine, a research consultant at the Massachusetts Institute of Technology's program on Internet and telecom convergence, has a reassuring analysis on the larger question of whether a few big companies are taking over the world's media. He believes that the 50 largest media companies in the United States account for little more of total media revenue than did the companies that made up the top 50 in 1986. "Media merger activity," says Compaine, "is more like rearranging the furniture." He argues that while the big media companies have grown larger over the past 15 years, so have the developed economies, "so expanding enterprises often are simply standing still in relative terms."

The United Nations' *Human Development Report 2002* concluded that 29 percent of the world's largest newspapers are state-owned and another 57 percent are family-owned. Only 8 percent are owned by employees or the public. For radio, 72 percent are state-owned and 24 percent family-owned. Sixty percent of television stations are state-owned and 34 percent family-owned. There is little direct investment in the media sector of most countries, Compaine concluded.

A few big companies are not taking over the world's media, he argues, nor do U.S. companies dominate the media. He also maintains that global media do not drown out local content. In Brazil, he notes, the

U.S. commercial network MTV "plays a mix of music, videos, and other programming determined by local producers, even though it shares a recognizable format with MTV stations elsewhere." Fostering competition, says Compaine, has long been a central goal of U.S. media regulation. He contends that stricter regulation is not in the public interest and even argues that relaxing U.S. broadcast regulation has led to more competition. For example, Fox launched a new network to compete with the traditional three big networks (NBC, CBS, and ABC), and several other new networks have emerged under deregulation.

For poor countries and the poor within rich countries, the principal issue is greater access to the global media. To move the world toward this objective is the stated goal of the World Summit on the Information Society (WSIS) scheduled for late 2003. One may hope, consequently, that the WSIS will not support restrictions on the Internet, but will encourage the widest possible diversity.

Conclusion

What, then, are the prospects that the Internet as well as more traditional news media will experience real freedom while providing more diverse flows of news and information?

The primary answer rests in the democratizing function of news media. In the past quarter century, news and information flows markedly influenced political change throughout the world. Democratic governance, after all, is impossible without a free press. However, an unstable democratic government (or any other unstable system) generally leads to restrictions on the press. A hopeful sign is the increasing awareness of this correlation and the growing number of places where freer mass communications, including the Internet, are slowly putting down stronger and more permanent roots. The emphasis placed on human rights by the United States and other governments also has had a positive impact. Despite horrendous violations of human rights in recent years, a higher standard for treatment of the press is becoming the norm.

The imposition by governments of "a new information order" has been defeated. That is a start. To be recognized as a genuine democracy, a country must remove the barriers to freedom of the news media. At the same time, the press is expected to fulfill its journalistic responsibilities as an essential part of a free society. That commitment requires diverse reportorial, editorial, and analytical coverage of domestic and international affairs, interaction between the public and the press, and the accessibility of the media to the information-poor—all without distortions of truth by sensationalism or bias.

The past quarter century has seen both a global assault on press freedom and a remarkable gain for freedom of the news media. The great challenge for the press freedom movement is to maintain vigilance—lest progress be reversed—and expand a free press reach where the censor still prevails.

A New Opening for Press Controllers

Ronald Koven

In the name of protecting national security a serious challenge to a free press looms. The battleground, both in December 2003 and again in 2005, will be the International Telecommunication Union (ITU), the world's oldest intergovernmental organization. The ITU for nearly a century has regulated communications as they related principally to spectrum assignments. Now it contemplates regulation of international Internet and broadcast content.

When the ITU decided in 1998 to organize a UN system conference to be called the World Summit on the Information Society (WSIS), I, as well as members of other civil society groups, thought it inevitable that frustrated advocates of the controversial New World Information and Communication Order (NWICO) would use the WSIS to try again to control the world's press. This time, they could feed on the new anxieties created among both democratic and nondemocratic authorities over the advent of the Internet and direct satellite broadcasting, and their potential use by terrorists.

Preparations for the World Summit were in midstream as the United States—which has been the leading governmental advocate of press freedom in the international arena and the main opponent of NWICO—was attacked on September 11, 2001, by a radically new form of terrorism. The U.S. government's attachment to press freedom was overshadowed

Ronald Koven is the European Representative of the World Press Freedom Committee, and has held major editing and/or reporting positions at the International Herald Tribune, Washington Post and Boston Globe. He was a participant in the preparatory conference for the World Summit on the Information Society.

by its new concerns for national security. An American government that had championed the opportunities offered by the "information superhighways" now joined the ranks of the anxious, fearful of the dimly understood possibilities of the new technologies.

These concerns about terrorism, as well as such "harmful content" issues as child pornography, may lead democratic governments to join with authoritarians who seek greater state controls over the Internet.

This trend was made manifest in the fall and winter of 2002–2003 in a series of government-dominated meetings in Geneva, Bucharest, Tokyo, Beirut, Paris, and Amsterdam. A European regional conference on the WSIS held in Bucharest, Romania, on November 7–9, 2002 (the meeting included the United States, Canada, and Israel) concluded with a declaration warning that the Internet could be used to weaken "international stability and security."

In the second half of February 2003, two full weeks of meetings in Geneva of the second preparatory conference (PrepCom 2) of WSIS ended inconclusively, with texts under consideration containing a large number of concepts traditionally dear to would-be press controllers. These include the "right to communicate," "balancing" information flows, and informational respect for "national sovereignty." The need for "security" in cyberspace was at the top of the U.S. government agenda. The latest available WSIS Draft Action Plan, issued March 21, 2003, called for "creating a rapid reaction organization to deal with security violations," as well as "studying the long-term possibility of creating an international convention on the security of information and communication networks."

U.S. diplomats at the Bucharest meeting said they shared in the security concerns of their colleagues and that they were satisfied with a final declaration that made a bow to "the need to preserve the free flow of information" but contained language placing security concerns uppermost, including a call to develop "a global culture of cyber-security." By February, when the entire governmental membership of the UN system took part in Geneva in the second of three world preparatory conferences for WSIS, even that weak recognition of the free flow of information had disappeared.

At the Bucharest conference, in the palace built by the late Romanian dictator Nicolae Ceaucescu to rival the Pentagon as the world's largest building, press freedom groups spoke out against a governmental draft. However, these groups were not allowed to participate in the negotiations over the language of the draft declaration; participants were limited to representatives of 55 governments including most of the industrialized world. While the United Nations has called for inclusion of civil society groups as full partners in WSIS, governments have been holding nongovernmental organizations at arm's length.

The European governments did include in their first paragraph positive language echoing Article 19 of the Universal Declaration of Human Rights (UDHR): "The European regional conference proposes the vision of an Information Society, where all persons, without distinction of any kind, exercise their right to freedom of opinion and expression, including the freedom to hold opinions without interference, and to seek, receive and impart information and ideas through any media and regardless of frontiers." However, government representatives resisted calls by press freedom groups to specify that that language comes almost word for word from the UDHR. Such attribution would have had the effect of emphasizing the universal nature of press freedom.

Yoshio Utsumi, secretary-general of the Geneva-based International Telecommunication Union, the lead UN agency preparing WSIS, advanced an even more ambitious regulatory approach. He said in Bucharest that "cyberspace is a new land without frontiers and without a government yet." He then asked, "Who can police cyberspace and how?" and he answered that a "new global government" is needed to police and control crime, security, taxation, and privacy in cyberspace.

The ITU's approach seemed to reflect an attempt to find a major new role for itself as a regulatory agency, in a world communication-technology environment where its importance had been diminishing, thanks to deregulation. Conference arrangements seemed designed to stress ITU's lead role while minimizing that of other concerned UN agencies, such as UNESCO. "It's all about elbowing out any competition," said an official U.S. source.

The governmental drive for regulation of the Internet also got a big boost when the annual meeting of the board of ICANN, the Internet Corporation for Assigned Names and Numbers, meeting in Amsterdam on December 14–15, 2002, adopted new governance rules. Under these rules, its structure was transformed from an almost purely self-regulatory system without government interference into one that includes a virtual veto by representatives of states acting collectively in a Government Advisory Committee whose "recommendations" can now be ignored with great difficulty.

The new ICANN system lays the groundwork for a reassertion of "national information sovereignty" over the use of national domain names.

What this can lead to is illustrated by China's creation of a national Internet that does not interact with foreign networks. Already, a number of Chinese Internet users have been jailed for downloading or distributing "subversive" messages. Such offenses are detected by a corps of tens of thousands of monitors who follow what Chinese users do on the Internet.

Meanwhile, a seminar organized by the French National Commission for UNESCO, held on November 15–16, 2002, also stressed governmental regulation. In opening the Paris meeting, "Freedom of Expression in the Information Society," French National Commission president Jean Favier said, "If proclaiming freedom is easy to do, it is more difficult to outline its contours. As we know, these are made up of restrictions."

He spoke of the need to control hate speech, racial discrimination, pornography, and pedophilia, as well as the need to protect privacy. "The authorities put in place to guarantee the regulation of the media ... are still deprived of any effective means of control" in an environment where information can circulate anonymously and there is no right of reply, he said. Talk of "cyber-terrorism and cyber-criminality" are no exaggerations, he added. Favier was echoed in this approach by the chief of the Media Section of the Strasbourg-based Council of Europe.

Americans attending the meeting were stunned by the extent to which Europeans have come to view the First Amendment of the U.S. Constitution as a "problem" standing in the way of regulating "hate speech" and other "harmful content." The notion of "illegal content" is one that American lawyers have no trouble dealing with, but the introduction of a subjective concept like "harmful content," a growingly popular approach at the Council of Europe, leaves American jurists deeply troubled.

Meeting in Vienna this fall, the coordinating committee of nine leading press freedom organizations adopted a joint position that no content regulation or any other special press laws are needed for the Internet. The committee called for worldwide implementation of Article 19 and for reaffirmation of UNESCO's Sofia Declaration that news media using new technology should have "the same freedom of expression protections as traditional media."

This Vienna Declaration was adopted by the Committee to Protect Journalists (New York), the Commonwealth Press Union (London), the Inter American Press Association (Miami), the International Association of Broadcasting (Montevideo, Uruguay), the International Federation of the Periodical Press (London), the International Press Institute (Vienna), the North American Broadcasters Association (Ottawa), the World Association of Newspapers (Paris), and the World Press Freedom Committee (Washington, D.C.).

The latest available WSIS texts—working documents issued March 21, 2003, and based on extracts from declarations adopted by African, European, Latin American-Caribbean, Asian-Pacific and West Asian regional meetings—were open to further comment before a new, previously unscheduled, "intersession" negotiation, set for July 15–18, 2003, was to be held at UNESCO Headquarters in Paris. On the basis of experience to date, however, the expectations were that this additional session could well fail to produce consensus texts and that negotiations would continue into PrepCom 3, September 17–28, 2003, most probably in Geneva.

PrepCom 2 was attended by 1,535 participants, nearly 900 of whom were members of governmental delegations and nearly 400 of whom were from nongovernmental organizations and "civil society."

A diverse group of nongovernmental organizations that has been following WSIS has petitioned against holding a second summit in Tunisia because of that country's active repression of press freedom. As of March 2003, the editor of a Tunisian Internet magazine had been in prison for six months for writing that the Tunisian government has prevented the independence of the country's judiciary.

From the start, the PrepCom and related meetings were bedeviled by gavel-to-gavel procedural wrangling, spearheaded by Pakistan with strong backing from China, Cuba, Libya, and Syria. These countries have worked from the outset to confine proceedings and internal negotiations, as much as possible, to governments—excluding civil society nongovernmental organizations and the private sector groups and corporations with which the ITU has traditionally worked.

The governmental delegations decided that proposals from nongovernmental groups would be circulated in a separate annex, which suggests that such proposals could have a hard time being incorporated into the final documents.

A text put together by a "Content and Themes Drafting Group" tightly controlled by militants of the radical CRIS (Communication Rights in the Information Society) campaign was a grabbag of extreme demands—but it also included some suggestions from a caucus of mostly mainstream journalistic nongovernmental organizations. Consequently, in a last-minute decision that media caucus sought to concentrate on direct communication with the WSIS organizers, rather than let its views be homogenized into the CRIS-dominated arrangement for input at WSIS.

Another worrying feature of the latest drafts was the repeated attempt to hem in approving calls for "independent and free communication media" with the qualifier "in accordance with the legal system of each country." This approach was picked up from the Asian-Pacific regional group's Tokyo Declaration of January 2003 and reflects China's insistence on respect for "national information sovereignty."

Another idea harking back to the New World Information and Communication Order (NWICO) goals was the idea of needing to "balance" information flows. That phrase was used in the 1980s as, among other things, a NWICO rallying cry against the alleged domination of world news by the major Western news agencies.

A broad suggestion of the kind of denial of the universality of human rights embodied in the "Asian values" approach is also contained in a call to "facilitate" the "development of compatible regulations and standards that respect national characteristics and concerns."

The Civil Society Secretariat, specially created for the WSIS preparations, was apparently tasked with trying to see that the actual Summit would not be marred by violent street demonstrations, as had happened to major international meetings in Seattle, Genoa, and elsewhere. The Secretariat's approach was that it was better to have CRIS inside the process than on the outside making trouble. CRIS is led by an Irishman named Sean O'Siochru, a former secretary-general of the MacBride Roundtable, named for the late Irish foreign minister Sean MacBride, head of UNESCO's NWICO-era MacBride Commission.

CRIS effectively penetrated the WSIS preparatory process, notably by establishing close relations with the ITU early in the UN agency's Summit planning. A fulltime CRIS coordinator was housed in the London offices of the World Association for Christian Communication (WACC). Other leading CRIS member organizations included AMARC (the French acronym for "World Association of Artisans of Community Radios"), the Association for Progressive Communication, the MacBride Roundtable, the People's Communication Charter, and the Inter Press Service, a radical news agency, as well as a long list of veteran NWICO ideologues led by Dutch professor Cees Hamelink, the leading advocate of the CRIS-adopted ideology of a "right to communicate." CRIS has varied between a very ideological presentation of its agenda and a bland, consensual one, depending on circumstances and target audiences.

Apparently to water down the influence of CRIS, the Civil Society Secretariat arranged for the creation shortly before PrepCom 2 of a Civil Society Bureau whose function was to interact with the WSIS's official bureau of ITU member-state delegates. The Secretariat suggested that civil society be broken into a dozen "families," each of which would have a Civil Society Bureau representative. These included a "Media Family" of press freedom groups, unions, academics, etc. O'Siochru joined the bureau as the representative for the "Social Movements Family."

Evidently realizing that he and his allies would be outnumbered in such a body, O'Siochru adamantly insisted that the bureau and its members, renamed "focal points," should be responsible solely for procedural questions and that substance would be the domain of a CRIS-run "Content and Themes Drafting Group." CRIS advocates also insisted that the number of "families" represented in the bureau should be open-ended.

To counteract the mainstream organizations of the "Media Family," CRIS fostered the creation of a "Communication Rights Family," an "Information Networks Family," and a "Community Media Family." I was elected "focal point" of the "Media Family," with Jacques Briquemont of the European Broadcasting Union and Tracey Naughton of the Media Institute of Southern Africa as "alternates." O'Siochru loudly objected during PrepCom 2 that a 30-strong meeting of the "Media Family" had enjoyed no standing to produce a text of its own. The "Media Family" had to agree that it would not speak as a "Family" but with a different hat, as a "Media Caucus."

When, on the last day of PrepCom 2, it came time to incorporate a modest list of "Media Caucus" proposals into the Civil Society Secretariat draft proposals for the WSIS Action Plan, the Content and Themes Drafting Group interspersed them without identifying their source in a very long document overwhelmed by a large number of proposals from the "Community Media Family" group.

So, the last meeting of the "Media Caucus"—with representatives of the International Association of Broadcasting, the International Federation of Journalists, Media Action International, the World Press Freedom Committee, and the World Radio and Television Council—agreed that in future the media group should submit any texts directly to the WSIS organizers, without going through a Civil Society drafting process biased against the mainstream news media groups.

Professor Hamelink was the lead speaker at a special public workshop on media at PrepCom 2, February 21, 2003, entitled "Right to Communicate vs. Freedom of Expression in the Information Society." Intervening right after Hamelink, I argued that there already is a "right to communicate" embodied in the UDHR's Article 19 and that what is needed is its implementation. Citing a recent Hamelink outline of the "right to communicate" in the WACC quarterly magazine *Media Development*, I illustrated how a number of Hamelink's ideas play into authoritarian hands. Toby Mendel of Canada, the Law Program director of the London-based group Article 19, outlined a lengthy and negative critique of Hamelink's detailed exposition of a "right to communicate." A large audience clearly leaned against the "right to communicate" approach. Among those speaking against it from the audience were Western governmental delegates who said this is no time to try to define a new right.

Even before the workshop, there was a major public clash over "right to communicate" when I contested a CRIS speaker advocating it from an official WSIS platform. I described it as a potential cover for censorship. A Cuban delegate immediately backed CRIS. Several participants later said that Cuba's support for CRIS had in effect confirmed my analysis.

The mood against the "right to communicate" was running so strong that a leading CRIS member, Professor William McIver, of the State University of New York at Albany, said he saw a need to rethink the whole issue. Anriette Esterhuysen, the South African executive director of the Association for Progressive Communication, said she had found the arguments against "right to communicate" most convincing because so many of the proposals associated with it recall her own country's apartheid-era laws.

In response, Sean O'Siochru, however, unveiled plans for CRIS to hold a one-day "Communication Rights Summit" parallel to the WSIS meeting in December. A paper issued by O'Siochru said his personal summit would be the "culmination" of "a series of workshops, thematic debates, drafting activities, online events [and] will be supported by publications and electronic fora."

Clearly, fundamental issues are at stake in the forthcoming World Summits on the Information Society. Not least are the efforts of some governments and radical nongovernmental organizations nostalgic for NWICO to regulate the content of domestic and international news and information flows over the Internet. However noble the declared objectives, such as assuring national security, attempts to control content on the Internet could, if successful, serve as new openings to revisit the kind of international censorship regimes that democratic government fought off during the Cold War. However, the threats some democracies now fear from the Internet seem to have desensitized them to the dangers to press freedom from such autocratic regimes.

The official draft's call for a "global culture of cyber-security" is a clear warning that important freedoms are under challenge. It would be a sad day indeed if, when the WSIS convenes in December, the world's democracies should join with authoritarian states to legitimate ideas that could set back the cause of press freedom.

Free Press in Russia and Ukraine: A Key to Integration into Europe

Thomas A. Dine

A free press is critical in bridging the historic and societal differences between East and West. While democracy has spread eastward in recent years, its roots are not yet deep. Even in Poland, Hungary, and the Czech Republic, which have entered NATO and will soon join the EU, the press is more often pluralist than free. Media outlets seek to advance the political or business interests of their patrons, rather than to publish the truth. However, it is in the two biggest fish in the former Soviet sea—Russia and Ukraine—where one can see the most tortuous and ambivalent search for a European identity and values, as well as the biggest disparity between rhetoric and reality, between words and actions. While Russian president Vladimir Putin and Ukrainian president Leonid Kuchma both proclaim that the key to their nations' futures lies with integration into the democratic West, both leaders routinely demonstrate indifference towards, and even contempt for, the first freedom upon which a functioning democracy depends: freedom of expression, a free press.

In Russia, President Putin, like a modern-day Peter the Great, has made integration with the West a centerpiece of his foreign policy. To his credit, he has backed up that assertion since the attacks of September 11 by providing the United States with much-needed support in the war on

Thomas A. Dine is President of Radio Free Europe/Radio Liberty. This essay was originally delivered as a speech at the Freedom House conference "Bridging the New East-West Divide: Russia and the Expanding Euro-Atlantic Community," Budapest, January 30, 2003.

terror. However, though Putin might be cooperating with the democracies of the West, he seems determined to preserve an iron fist at home.

Since assuming presidential power in 2000, Putin has demonstrated that he is a determined foe of an independent and free press. The Committee to Protect Journalists named Putin one of the "Ten Worst Enemies of the Press for 2001," and with good reason. He has gone to great lengths to obstruct accurate reporting from the war in Chechnya, which has had two harmful consequences. First, Russian soldiers, untroubled by any audience of television viewers or newspaper readers to hold them accountable for their actions, have been committing unspeakable acts against the Chechen population. Second, the Russian people, whose opposition to the first Chechen war played an instrumental role in ending it, and who have been asked to give their lives, or the lives of their husbands, sons, and fathers, for this equally futile second Chechen war, have very little idea of the brutality taking place in the North Caucasus.

Putin has demonstrated a determination to silence as many independent national media outlets as possible. Rather than using the old-fashioned Soviet methods of censorship, he has relied upon a more subtle, but highly effective, method: business. In the past two years, Putin has brought the NTV television network, the Ekho Moskvy radio network, the weekly magazine *Itogi*, and the newspaper *Segodnya*—all of which were much-needed voices of independence in the landscape of Russian media—under the influence of the government. In each case, this was accomplished not through Soviet-style censorship, but through the deft manipulation of commercial levers.

Russian journalists are definitely getting the message that Putin is no friend of theirs. Two years ago, 15 days after Putin became president, Radio Free Europe/Radio Liberty (RFE/RL) reporter Andrei Babitsky was kidnapped by Russian soldiers in Chechnya in blatant retaliation for his unsparing reports about the first war and the first three months of the second war. Former U.S. Deputy Secretary of State Strobe Talbot writes that the Russian journalists he is in contact with confirm that Russia's president has introduced a chill on freedom of the press that is "huge and ominous." In January 2003, Putin's allies ousted business magnate Boris Jordan as head of the NTV television network, as an expression of the Kremlin's displeasure with NTV's coverage of the October hostage crisis in Moscow. In addition, there are several indications that the next media target of the Kremlin is RFE/RL. Radio Liberty faces an uphill battle to get its AM license in Moscow renewed by July 2003.

An equally troubling situation exists in Ukraine. President Kuchma, like Putin, claims that integration with the West is the key to his country's future security and prosperity. He expresses the desire that Ukraine should join the EU and NATO. However, like Putin, Kuchma has undermined these aspirations by cultivating decidedly nondemocratic practices against the Ukrainian press.

Ukraine, to put it mildly, is not a good place to be a journalist. Reporters there have more to fear than the censorship and intimidation that unfortunately plague much of the media in the former Soviet Union—Ukrainian journalists must also fear for their lives. In June 2001, a publisher was murdered; a month later, a director at an independent television station was bludgeoned to death. Although Kuchma himself may not be to blame for all the mayhem that is visited on reporters in his country, evidence exists, including a tape recording of a conversation in his office indicating involvement, that he is directly responsible for the most notorious act of violence against a Ukrainian journalist in recent memory: the beheading of Georgy Gongadze. It is little wonder, then, that Kuchma has joined Putin as one of the Committee to Protect Journalists' ten worst enemies of the press.

Kuchma's latest media target is RFE/RL. As a broadcast entity funded in the United States and produced in Prague, RFE/RL's Ukrainian service has not shied away from exposing the massive corruption in his administration. However, while Kuchma cannot go after RFE/RL, he can attack its affiliate station in Ukraine, and that is precisely what he has done. Radio Dovira, a nationwide FM news and music network, is RFE/RL's partner and the primary link to its Ukrainian listeners. Last year, the national TV and Radio Council told Dovira's executives that its days of carrying RFE/RL broadcasts are numbered. With allegations against him ranging from vote-stealing to illicit arms sales to Iraq, Kuchma simply cannot afford to have independent media outlets reporting straight news and airing vibrant, balanced commentary.

However, it is important to remember that not all the problems facing journalists in Russia and Ukraine can be laid at the feet of Putin and Kuchma. More and more, it is regional government officials who are behind the skulduggery that permeates the media environments in the former Soviet Union. Furthermore, many of the obstacles to press freedom are not overtly political in nature.

In the first place, practicing journalism in Russia and Ukraine entails enormous economic burdens. Low salaries are the rule. Expenses for computers, transmitters, newsprint, paper, and the like are onerous enough in a healthy economy; in Russia and Ukraine, they are downright debilitating. Private media outlets have a limited pool of advertisers from which to draw extra revenue, and therefore have a hard time turning a profit. When impoverished media employ impoverished journalists to report to an impoverished audience, the result is a journalistic climate that is conducive to corruption: people with money can get their stories told and their views expressed, while people without money cannot. Moneyed interests—including government officials—can manipulate coverage of their actions, as cash-starved newspapers are offered financial inducements to tell the payer's side of the story. Call it "journalistic bribery."

Journalists in Russia and Ukraine must also struggle with politically motivated actions by their legal systems. Indeed, the launching of criminal cases against journalists represents the biggest trend in the censorship industry in Russia. The three years of Putin's presidency have already witnessed more criminal cases against reporters than were seen during the 10 years of Yeltsin's rule. Government officials use libel lawsuits to harass reporters they do not like; tax police fine and in some cases bankrupt independent media outlets; local police seize computers as collateral against future fines; and even health inspectors shut down media outlets for not maintaining the proper room temperature in their offices.

Meanwhile, the prevalence of organized crime has made targets of journalists who dare to print the truth about corruption. In the last three years, according to the Moscow-based Glasnost Defense Fund, nearly 40 Russian journalists have been killed or have died under mysterious circumstances, and 4 others have disappeared. Regrettably, Russian authorities have shown little interest in solving these crimes, perhaps because the trail of culpability too often leads back into the boardroom, the police station, or the city hall. As we have seen with the Gongadze case, death and disappearances pervade the media environment in Ukraine as well; authorities regularly beat and harass reporters.

In a climate such as this, when independent journalists face everything from lawsuits to jail to death, it is almost a miracle that anyone is willing to do journalism at all. In fact, fewer and fewer are willing. The continued health of a free and independent press is hard enough to maintain in free societies—witness the increased hegemony wielded by Prime Minister Silvio Berlusconi over Italian television, or the scandal in Poland involving the ruling party's alleged attempt to bribe the publisher of a major Polish newspaper. The deck is especially stacked, however, against journalists in Russia and Ukraine.

There is, nevertheless, a significant glimmer of hope in all this: transnational bodies such as the World Trade Organization, the EU, and NATO. Despite the dismal media environment in Ukraine and Russia, Putin and Kuchma do want to join these organizations. However, if they think that they can integrate their countries into the West merely by being cooperative partners on the international stage—that as long as they support Western Europe and the United States in their foreign policies, they can pursue whatever domestic policies they like and still join the World Trade Organization, the EU, and NATO—they are sorely mistaken.

These transnational institutions to which Russia and Ukraine aspire are not content to look only at the candidate nation's behavior in the international arena. The EU has a dizzying list of requirements pertaining to human rights that each nation must meet before admission is even considered. NATO, which during the Cold War was content to overlook some autocratic behavior among its members, now seems determined to admit as new members only those countries that respect civil liberties and human rights. For those of us in the democracy-export business, the "nosiness" of these transnational organizations—their insistence on looking not merely at a candidate nation's external behavior but at its internal behavior as well—is one of the most hopeful developments in recent memory. Sometimes what cannot be accomplished by sticks (criticism from democratic governments and human rights organizations) can be accomplished by carrots (jobs and money).

A spectacular example of the "power of carrots" is the effort by Turkey to join the EU. Turkey knows that the EU is now the only game in town, economically. So, in order to meet the exhaustive requirements of the Acquis Communautaire—an 80,000-page body of laws, governing everything under the sun, that each EU member must adopt in its entirety—Turkey has made reforms that were simply unthinkable 10 years ago. It has abolished the death penalty. It has undone its long-standing prohibitions against teaching and broadcasting in the Kurdish language. It has removed clauses from its constitution that permitted incarcerating people for reciting "Islamicist" literature. It has even promised to put an end to the practice of torture in its police stations.

The government of Turkey did not make all these changes out of a sudden burst of altruism. It did so because it wants to join the EU. Thanks to the promise of prosperity that the EU offers, Turkey has been doing the hard work of transforming itself not merely into a society with free elections, but into a society that honors the individual freedoms that deepen democracy's roots. We can therefore breathe a sigh of relief that no matter how well the Kuchmas and Putins of this world behave on the international stage, their countries will never claim the prize of NATO or EU membership until they allow the media to report the news free from state obstruction. Keeping a lid on the press may make it easier for Putin to conduct the war in Chechnya and for Kuchma to line his pockets, but until Russia and Ukraine start practicing and protecting freedom of the press, their stated goals of integration into the West will remain unfulfilled fantasies.

We in the West must not let our attention stray from this issue. Many people in the West today mistakenly think that Russia and Ukraine are now free countries. It takes more than free elections to establish true democracy; it takes a range of civil institutions, including, above all, a free press. The process by which freedom of the press takes root is slow, gradual, and painful. It is, however, a process that is absolutely vital to democracy's ultimate success.

COUNTRY REPORTS AND RATINGS

Afghanistan

LEGAL ENVIRONMENT: 24
POLITICAL INFLUENCES: 30
ECONOMIC PRESSURES: 20

Status: Not Free

TOTAL SCORE: 74

Following the fall of the repressive Taliban regime in late 2001, conditions for Afghanistan's media improved markedly. A new press law adopted in February 2002 guaranteed the right to press freedom, but also contained a number of broadly worded restrictions on licensing, foreign ownership, and insult laws that could be subject to abuse. Authorities have granted more than 100 licenses to independent publications, although some regional warlords have refused to allow independent media outlets to operate in the areas under their control. In January, the independent publication *Kabul Weekly* started publishing after a suspension of five years. However, journalists in Kabul reported several instances of threats and harassment at the hands of authorities, according to the London-based Index on Censorship. Many avoid writing about sensitive issues such as Islam, national unity, or crimes committed by the warlords. Both Afghan and foreign reporters were also subjected to intimidation and physical attacks from regional warlords and their security services, the U.S. armed forces, or unidentified assailants. Television broadcasts were restored in November 2001 after a total ban under the Taliban. However, in August 2002, officials in Kabul banned the airing of Indian films on TV and ruled that radio stations must not broadcast women singing, and in December the Supreme Court banned cable television stations in the city of Jalalabad. The state owns a number of newspapers and almost all of the electronic news media.

Albania

LEGAL ENVIRONMENT: 20
POLITICAL INFLUENCES: 18
ECONOMIC PRESSURES: 12

Status: Partly Free

TOTAL SCORE: 50

Persistent attacks against journalists and a general climate of government intimidation remain the greatest threats to press freedom in Albania. Article 22 of the constitution bans censorship and guarantees freedom of the press. At times, the government acts to restrict these rights in practice. Journalists commonly experience official harassment, physical attacks, death threats, and other forms of intimidation. In October 2002, state officials singled out the daily *Koha Jone* for financial and labor inspections after the paper published critical remarks about Prime Minister Iliv Meta. Nearly all broadcast media in Albania are privately owned. While Albania Radio and Television (TVSH) legally became an independent public entity in 2000, its news coverage remains considerably pro-government. There are 15 private national daily newspapers and nearly 150 weekly and monthly publications. The high cost of production and limited advertising revenue continue to threaten the financial viability of many independent publications.

Algeria

Status: Not Free

LEGAL ENVIRONMENT: 21
POLITICAL INFLUENCES: 24
ECONOMIC PRESSURES: 17
TOTAL SCORE: 62

Algeria has a vibrant private press. Newspapers offer competing views, and reports critical of the government frequently appear in independent publications. However, press freedom remains constrained by government pressure and legal restrictions that lead some journalists to practice self-censorship. The penal code gives the government authority to impose high fines and jail sentences of up to two years in cases in which journalists "defame, insult, or injure" government officials or institutions. Under restrictive new laws, passed in 2001, that increased the monetary penalties for defamation, several independent journalists faced legal action and were sentenced to steep fines as well as prison terms during the year. Journalists often are the victims of intimidation, harassment and physical violence for criticizing public officials or other groups. Nevertheless, the situation has improved considerably since the 1990s, when reporters were the targets of Islamic insurgents. However, in 2002 a veteran journalist with a French-language television station was brutally killed. Radio and television are under government control, with coverage biased in favor of government policies. Tariffs on the importation of foreign publications were recently raised, so that total charges now amount to more than 25 percent of the cover price. Most independent newspapers rely on the state for printing and paper imports, and the government occasionally withholds advertising from newspapers on political grounds.

LEGAL ENVIRONMENT: 1
POLITICAL INFLUENCES: 1

Andorra

ECONOMIC PRESSURES: 6

Status: Free

TOTAL SCORE: 8

Media in the principality are free in principle and practice. Article 12 of the constitution bans censorship and guarantees freedom of expression. The Universal Declaration of Human Rights, which is binding in Andorra, likewise protects press freedom. The legal system provides for the right of reply in cases of slander. Two independent daily newspapers and several weeklies serve the country's 70,000 inhabitants. Andorra has two radio stations, one state-owned and one privately owned, and six television stations. Citizens can receive broadcasts from neighboring France and Spain.

LEGAL ENVIRONMENT: 20
POLITICAL INFLUENCES: 30

Angola

ECONOMIC PRESSURES: 22

Status: Not Free

TOTAL SCORE: 72

Following the death of UNITA leader Jonas Savimbi in February and the signing of a peace accord between the government and rebel fighters in March, conditions for the media eased somewhat in 2002. Although the constitution states that the media cannot be subjected to censorship, the government does not always respect this provision in practice. Defamation of the president or his representatives is a criminal offense punishable by imprisonment or fines. In January, a court ordered freelance journalist Rafael Marques to pay $950 as well as all legal costs pertaining to the trial, after he was found guilty of defaming President Jose Eduardo dos Santos in a 1999 article. Reporters continue to face various forms of official harassment, including the confiscation of travel documents and limitations on the right to travel; arbitrary arrest and detention; and physical attacks. While some journalists practice self-censorship when reporting on sensitive issues, the private print and broadcast media are generally free to scrutinize government policies. However, coverage at state-owned outlets favors the ruling party. The government has reportedly paid journalists to publish complimentary stories and has discouraged advertisers from buying space in independent newspapers, thus threatening their financial viability.

Antigua and Barbuda

Status: Partly Free

LEGAL ENVIRONMENT: 12
POLITICAL INFLUENCES: 16
ECONOMIC PRESSURES: 17
TOTAL SCORE: 45

Freedom of the press is provided for in the constitution. However, television and radio continue to be dominated by the ruling Antigua Labour Party (ALP) and the Bird family, which have ruled the country for more than four decades. At state-controlled broadcast media outlets, the government frequently sets the editorial policy. Print media are considered freer and more vibrant than broadcast media. The government limits the opposition's access to broadcast media and has in the past interfered with attempts by individuals to establish independent media sources. The country's first independent radio station, Observer Radio, began broadcasting in 2001 after a five-year struggle with the government to gain a license. Prime Minister Lester Bird filed a $3 million lawsuit against the Observer media group and opposition leader Baldwin Spencer for "libelous fabrications" in conjunction with the drug and sex offense accusations made against him and members of the government. The Declaration of Chapultepec on press freedoms was signed in 2002. Despite this, media ownership remains highly concentrated and economically dependent on the ALP and the state.

Argentina

Status: Partly Free

LEGAL ENVIRONMENT: 11
POLITICAL INFLUENCES: 16
ECONOMIC PRESSURES: 12
TOTAL SCORE: 39

The press is vibrant and highly active in serving as a watchdog by reporting on issues that limit press freedom in the country. Legally, press freedom is provided for in the constitution. However, libel is a criminal offense and is frequently used to harass journalists. In numerous cases, journalists were verbally intimidated and physically assaulted for carrying out their duties during the year. Most cases involved journalists who had reported on corruption involving government officials. The ongoing economic crisis has placed a heavy burden on print media, especially smaller independent newspapers. The government imposition of a value-added tax (VAT) on all media sales in 2001 has suffocated newspapers and put many in danger of collapse. Before the tax was imposed, print media were required to pay VAT only on advertising revenues. Losses in circulation and advertising revenues resulting from the new VAT requirements have drastically reduced the income of the print press. True press independence continues to be jeopardized by monthly stipends reportedly paid covertly by the state intelligence agency to dozens of reporters and editors, as well as by recent trends in the concentration of media ownership.

Armenia

Status: Not Free

LEGAL ENVIRONMENT: 23
POLITICAL INFLUENCES: 26
ECONOMIC PRESSURES: 16
TOTAL SCORE: 65

Status change explanation: Armenia's rating declined from Partly Free to Not Free as a result of the government's repeated use of security or criminal libel laws to stifle criticism, as well as the forced closing of the country's leading independent television station.

Freedom of the press declined in Armenia as a result of the closing of the country's leading independent television station, and the government's continued attempts to stifle criticism in the media. Article 24 of the constitution guarantees freedom of expression and the press. However, the government acts to limit these rights in practice. National security legislation and criminal libel laws allow the state to prosecute journalists for any perceived infraction. Journalists frequently experience physical assaults and other forms of intimidation in relation to their work. In late 2002, a reporter investigating the government's 1999 assault on the parliament building suffered serious injuries from a grenade attack. Law enforcement officials often decline to prosecute attacks against journalists. Most media outlets seek sponsorship from powerful business or political interests. These interests frequently exercise de facto editorial control over content and foster a climate of self-censorship among journalists. In April, the National Commission on Television and Radio transferred the broadcast frequency of A1+, the leading independent television station, to an entertainment company with reported links to the government. Often critical of the government, A1+ did not resume broadcasting in the run-up to presidential and parliamentary elections.

Australia

Status: Free

Legal Environment: 3
Political Influences: 5
Economic Pressures: 6
Total Score: 14

Although freedom of the press is generally respected, it is not expressly provided for in the constitution. In response to an outcry by press freedom groups, the government in March abandoned a proposal to criminalize the unauthorized disclosure or receipt of official information. The high court ruled in December that foreign media outlets could be sued for defamation in Australia for articles posted on the Internet, provided that the individual filing suit has a reputation to protect in the country. The novel ruling could undermine press freedom worldwide if copied by other countries. The independent Australian Press Council resolves complaints against the media. A journalist covering the detainee crisis at the Woomera detention center was briefly arrested in January, and unidentified gunmen fired shots into the home of an investigative reporter in October. Concentration of media ownership remains a concern.

Austria

Status: Free

Legal Environment: 11
Political Influences: 6
Economic Pressures: 6
Total Score: 23

Austrian media remained free in 2002. The federal constitution and the Media Law of 1981 provide the basis for a free press. Legal restrictions, although seldom invoked, forbid reporting deemed detrimental to morality or national security. Strict libel laws and the political use of libel lawsuits against journalists cloud coverage. The concentration of media ownership limits the pluralism of viewpoints and has raised antitrust concerns. Two media corporations, Mediaprint and Newsgroup, control the majority of newspapers and magazines. The state only recently began to issue private radio licenses, and government-controlled radio still dominants the airwaves. New legislation formally dissolved the state's television monopoly on January 1, 2002. Only one private television station has begun to compete with the state broadcaster. Internet access is unrestricted and widely available.

LEGAL ENVIRONMENT: 22
POLITICAL INFLUENCES: 28

Azerbaijan

ECONOMIC PRESSURES: 23

Status: Not Free

TOTAL SCORE: 73

The passage of new media legislation has had a positive influence on press freedom. Nevertheless, political interference and harsh economic conditions remain obstacles to the further development of free media in the country. Amendments to the Law on Mass Media came into effect in March 2002. Leading Azerbaijani press organizations applauded this development, as the amendments removed nearly all the registration requirements previously used to stifle print media. Existing laws governing television and radio broadcasting stand in contrast to these changes. President Heydar Aliev has the sole power to appoint members to the broadcast regulatory board. Ill-defined licensing procedures limit the growth of Azerbaijan's few independent broadcasters. Government lawsuits for libel threaten media outlets with severe fines and the prospect of closure. Many businesses are reluctant to pay for advertising in opposition media for fear of government reprisals. A government scheme to provide loans to struggling papers allows even greater room for political influence over the financially burdened independent press.

LEGAL ENVIRONMENT: 3
POLITICAL INFLUENCES: 3

Bahamas

ECONOMIC PRESSURES: 5

Status: Free

TOTAL SCORE: 11

Citizens of the Bahamas continue to enjoy press freedom, which is provided for in the constitution. Although libel laws exist, the government does not enforce these laws. There are several privately owned newspapers and radio stations that provide a variety of political opinions and are free to scrutinize the government and its policies. The state-owned Broadcasting Corporation of the Bahamas is the country's only television station. However, it is, for the most part, free of government influence and offers a wide variety of views. Some opposition parties have claimed that their viewpoints do not receive as much coverage as those of the ruling party. In a notable move, Prime Minister Hubert A. Ingraham signed the Declaration of Chapultepec, promising to support and promote press freedom in the country.

Bahrain

Status: Not Free

LEGAL ENVIRONMENT: 20
POLITICAL INFLUENCES: 25
ECONOMIC PRESSURES: 23
TOTAL SCORE: 68

Criticism in the press of government policies and the expression of opinions on social and economic issues has increased in recent years. A press law guarantees the right of journalists to operate independently and to publish information. However, it is still illegal to criticize the ruling family or the Saudi royal family, or to write articles that promote sectarian divisions. A November 2002 press law limited the state's capacity to close down publications arbitrarily, but vaguely worded provisions of the new law prohibiting activities such as the "propagation of immoral behavior" leave the door open for state pressure on the media. The government owns and operates all radio and television stations in the country, and these outlets provide only official views. Print media are privately owned, but they usually exercise self-censorship in articles covering sensitive topics. Satellite television is available, but it does not provide access to the Qatar–based news channel Al-Jazeera, which is widely available throughout the Middle East and North Africa.

Bangladesh

Status: Not Free

LEGAL ENVIRONMENT: 17
POLITICAL INFLUENCES: 31
ECONOMIC PRESSURES: 17
TOTAL SCORE: 65

Conditions for the press worsened in 2002. Although the constitution provides for freedom of expression subject to "reasonable restrictions," the press is constrained by national security legislation as well as sedition and criminal libel laws. In July, authorities withdrew the publishing license of an opposition daily, and issues of several foreign publications were banned or censored during the course of the year. Journalists face considerable pressure from organized crime groups, political activists, the government, and Islamic fundamentalists. In a June report, Reporters Sans Frontieres alleged that Bangladesh had the highest incidence worldwide of violence against the press. A reporter was murdered in March, and journalists are frequently the targets of death threats and violent attacks as a result of their coverage of corruption, criminal activity, and human rights abuses. In December, a number of foreign and local reporters were arrested, detained by security forces, and tortured while in custody after they attempted to report on the rise of Islamic fundamentalism. The independent print media present diverse views, but journalists practice some self-censorship. The state owns most broadcast media, and coverage favors the ruling party. Ekushey Television, the country's only independent terrestrial broadcaster, was forced to close in August after the Supreme Court upheld the withdrawal of its license. Political considerations influence the distribution of government advertising revenue and subsidized newsprint, upon which most publications are dependent.

Barbados

Status: Free

LEGAL ENVIRONMENT: 1
POLITICAL INFLUENCES: 4
ECONOMIC PRESSURES: 9
TOTAL SCORE: 14

Freedom of the press is unrestricted, and the media are free of censorship and government control. The constitution provides for freedom of the press, and this right is respected in practice. The two major daily newspapers are privately owned, and there is a mix of private and public radio stations in operation. The state-owned Caribbean Broadcasting Corporation, which is the country's sole television station, represents a wide range of political views. There have been some complaints, however, that the government uses its influence to limit reporting on certain sensitive issues. There is some concentration of nongovernmental media ownership, but no other significant economic influences restrict press freedom.

Belarus

Status: Not Free

LEGAL ENVIRONMENT: 27
POLITICAL INFLUENCES: 32
ECONOMIC PRESSURES: 23
TOTAL SCORE: 82

The authoritarian regime of President Alyaksandr Lukashenka is openly hostile to a free press. New security legislation allows state agencies to effectively seize control of all media outlets under cover of counter-terrorism operations. This legislation prohibits press discussion of law enforcement activities and defines some forms of political protest as "terrorist" activity. In 2002, Belarusian courts sentenced Mikola Markevich, editor of the independent weekly *Pahonya*, and the journalist Pavel Mazheika to two years of forced labor for insulting the honor of the president. The sentence was reduced to one year on appeal. Authorities subsequently arrested 14 journalists for protesting in support of Markevich and Mazheika. State-run media outlets are subordinated to the president, whose regime controls press content and the appointment of senior editors. While state-controlled print and broadcast media do not offer a plurality of views, some regional television broadcasters cautiously attempt more balanced reporting. Many Belarusians receive their news from Russian television. However, the government is reportedly planning to assign the current Russian broadcast frequency to a new state television channel.

Belgium

Status: Free

LEGAL ENVIRONMENT: 3
POLITICAL INFLUENCES: 1
ECONOMIC PRESSURES: 5
TOTAL SCORE: 9

Belgian media enjoy strong constitutional protections for a free press. Restrictions on libel, pornography, and the promotion of racial or religious discrimination have only a minor effect on press freedom. In 2002, a court fined two journalists from the newspaper *De Morgen* for refusing to disclose confidential sources relating to a story on state railway cost overruns. Dual oversight boards seek to maintain balanced reporting on government-controlled radio and television networks. A handful of media corporations control the majority of newspapers.

Belize

Status: Free

LEGAL ENVIRONMENT: 11
POLITICAL INFLUENCES: 8
ECONOMIC PRESSURES: 4
TOTAL SCORE: 23

The constitution provides for freedom of the press, and the media operate freely, without regular interference by the government. The constitution, however, also stipulates that authorities have the right to intervene in media operations if the interests of national security, public order, or morality are at stake, though such intervention rarely occurs. Nevertheless, those who question the validity of financial disclosure statements submitted by public officials can be sentenced to prison terms of up to three years. Libel laws constrain freedom of expression, which encourages some self-censorship. However, a wide variety of viewpoints are still presented in the media. There are no daily newspapers, though there are several privately owned weekly papers and a large number of privately owned radio and television stations. The Belize Broadcasting Authority, a state-regulated agency, has the right to preview and censor certain broadcasts, including those with political content.

Benin
Status: Free

LEGAL ENVIRONMENT: 7
POLITICAL INFLUENCES: 11
ECONOMIC PRESSURES: 10
TOTAL SCORE: 28

Constitutional guarantees of freedom of expression are largely respected in practice. However, a 1997 criminal libel law remains on the books and has occasionally been used against journalists. The High Authority for Audio-Visual Communications, a government entity, is responsible for overseeing the operations of the media. Nevertheless, an independent and pluralistic press publishes articles highly critical of both government and opposition leaders and policies. Benin has a growing number of private newspapers and periodicals, more than 30 radio stations, and two television stations. However, the media remain subject to economic pressures. Journalists are poorly paid, and some are reportedly susceptible to bribery.

Bhutan
Status: Not Free

LEGAL ENVIRONMENT: 26
POLITICAL INFLUENCES: 25
ECONOMIC PRESSURES: 19
TOTAL SCORE: 70

The government prohibits criticism of King Wangchuk and Bhutan's political system, and authorities sharply restrict freedom of expression and the press. Bhutan's only regular publication, the private weekly *Kuensel*, reports news that puts the kingdom in a favorable light. The only exception is occasional coverage of criticism by National Assembly members of government policies during assembly meetings. Similarly, the state-run broadcast media do not carry opposition positions and statements. Cable television service, which carries uncensored foreign programming, thrives in some areas but is hampered by a high sales tax and the absence of a broadcasting law.

Bolivia

Status: Free

LEGAL ENVIRONMENT: 8
POLITICAL INFLUENCES: 14
ECONOMIC PRESSURES: 8
TOTAL SCORE: 30

In 2002, President Jorge Quiroga signed the Declaration of Chapultepec, promising to support and promote press freedom in the country. The constitution provides for freedom of the press. However, journalists are constrained by strict defamation and slander laws that carry sentences of up to three years' imprisonment. As a result, many journalists practice self-censorship. Journalists must be licensed by the government and must hold a university degree in order to practice their profession. Reporters covering corruption stories have been known to face verbal intimidation by government officials, arbitrary detention by police, and violent assaults. One journalist was murdered this year after a bomb exploded in the back seat of her car, although the motive is unknown. Newspapers are privately owned, and there is a mix of state and privately run radio and television stations. In practice, state advertising revenues often go to newspapers that are favorable to the government.

Bosnia-Herzegovina

Status: Partly Free

LEGAL ENVIRONMENT: 8
POLITICAL INFLUENCES: 20
ECONOMIC PRESSURES: 21
TOTAL SCORE: 49

Political influence in the media remains one of the largest impediments to the development of a truly free press in Bosnia. The constitution and the human rights annex to the Dayton peace accords provide the legal framework for a free press in the country. Parliamentary approval of a new defamation law in 2002 limited the threat of politically motivated defamation suits. However, government intervention and direct political patronage continue to restrict editorial independence. Journalists often experience death threats and physical attacks, especially when investigating war crimes. The 2002 Law on Public Broadcasting attempted to increase the independence of public broadcasters. Yet, critics have charged that the weaknesses in the law could allow for political influence in appointments to the broadcast oversight board.

	LEGAL ENVIRONMENT: 6
	POLITICAL INFLUENCES: 13
Botswana	ECONOMIC PRESSURES: 11
Status: Free	TOTAL SCORE: 30

Freedom of expression is provided for in the constitution and is generally respected, but the government imposes some limits on the press. Undesirable news stories and sources are subject to censorship, and several libel suits have been filed against members of the press in recent years. In November, an independent, self-regulatory press council was established. Although the private press is lively and is generally able to scrutinize the government, news coverage in the state-owned media supports official policies and actions. In addition, the opposition has alleged that it receives insufficient access to government-controlled media outlets. Several journalists were threatened or attacked during the year in retaliation for their critical reporting. In recent years, the government has used advertising bans in order to punish independent media outlets.

	LEGAL ENVIRONMENT: 11
	POLITICAL INFLUENCES: 18
Brazil	ECONOMIC PRESSURES: 9
Status: Partly Free	TOTAL SCORE: 38

Brazil is South America's largest media market with thousands of radio stations and hundreds of television stations across the country. The press is vigorous and commonly reports on controversial political and social issues. Nevertheless, press freedom was subjected to several constraints during the year. A 1967 law left over from the military dictatorship makes libel a criminal offense punishable by prison terms or fines. Although prison terms are rarely handed down, large fines can financially cripple news organizations. The courts are also used to censor the press in cases brought against journalists and media outlets by politicians and businessmen. Brazil's National Association of Journalists reported censorship to be at its highest levels since the 1964–1985 dictatorship. In addition, there were some instances of harassment and violence directed toward the press. Two journalists were murdered during the year, allegedly for investigating drug trafficking and corruption. However, arrests were made in both cases. Media ownership remains highly concentrated, and many news organizations have close ties to political parties and government officials. In a positive development, the media overall played a much less narrowly partisan and self-interested role during the 2002 presidential campaign than in past elections.

Brunei

Status: Not Free

LEGAL ENVIRONMENT: 28
POLITICAL INFLUENCES: 26
ECONOMIC PRESSURES: 22
TOTAL SCORE: 76

Freedom of the press is not provided for by law and is significantly restricted in practice. Legislation that took effect in October 2001 further restricts the rights of the media by requiring newspapers to apply for annual publishing permits, allowing officials to shut down newspapers without showing cause, threatening journalists with jail terms for publishing "false news," and requiring noncitizens to obtain government approval before working for the media. Private newspapers are owned or controlled by the sultan's family, or generally practice self-censorship on sensitive issues. However, several dailies do carry letters that criticize government policies. The only local broadcast media are operated by the government-controlled Radio Television Brunei, although cable television is available. There are no apparent restrictions on Internet use.

Bulgaria

Status: Free

LEGAL ENVIRONMENT: 10
POLITICAL INFLUENCES: 8
ECONOMIC PRESSURES: 12
TOTAL SCORE: 30

Although the press remains lively and diverse, press freedom declined for a second year as a result of continued government efforts to influence state and private media. Libel is a criminal offense and carries substantial fines. After taking power in 2001, the government of Prime Minister Simeon Saxecoburggotski expanded upon the previous government's practice of official interference in the operations of print and broadcast media. In October, parliament removed the director of the state news agency for an alleged lack of loyalty to the new ruling party. A similar shake-up had occurred at the state television network in December 2001. Later in the year, the prime minister's office announced that monthly press briefings would be closed to all but four radio and television stations, two of which would be state-run outlets. While the government directed advertising revenue to friendly media, financial pressures forced the closing of the opposition daily *Demokratsiya*. Political appointees to the new Electronic Media Council (EMC) will now oversee programming and issue broadcast licenses. The Council of Europe has expressed concern that the EMC could further weaken the editorial independence of state television and radio.

Burkina Faso
Status: Partly Free

LEGAL ENVIRONMENT: 9
POLITICAL INFLUENCES: 17
ECONOMIC PRESSURES: 13
TOTAL SCORE: 39

Freedom of speech is protected by the constitution and generally respected in practice. However, under the 1993 information code, media outlets accused of endangering national security or distributing false news can be summarily banned. The Supreme Council on Information, a state-run media supervisory body, regulates the broadcast media. Numerous independent publications, radio stations, and a private television station function with little governmental interference and are often highly critical of the government. Nevertheless, the administration remains sensitive to scrutiny and some journalists practice self-censorship. Reporters are occasionally subject to harassment and detention at the hands of police. Despite sustained public demand for an investigation into the 1998 murder of prominent journalist Norbert Zongo, his killers have not yet been charged and prosecuted.

Burma (Myanmar)

Status: Not Free

LEGAL ENVIRONMENT: 30
POLITICAL INFLUENCES: 37
ECONOMIC PRESSURES: 27
TOTAL SCORE: 94

The military junta sharply restricts press freedom. Legal restrictions on freedom of speech include a ban on statements that "undermine national security" and a stringent licensing system. Other decrees criminalize the possession and use of unregistered telephones, fax machines, computers and modems, and software. The government owns all broadcast media and daily newspapers and exercises tight control over a growing number of private weekly and monthly publications. It subjects private periodicals to prepublication censorship, and limits coverage to a small range of permissible topics. During the year, a number of publications were banned when they failed to comply with official regulations. In May, the junta also banned Thai advertising in the media, a move that threatened the financial viability of privately owned publications. Self-censorship is common. According to the Committee to Protect Journalists, international correspondents are generally not allowed to establish a base in Burma, and foreign reporters, who must apply for special visas to enter the country, are subject to intense scrutiny. In October, dozens of dissidents were arrested and detained for the possession of banned newspapers. Although several journalists were released from prison in 2002, more than a dozen remain incarcerated.

Burundi

Status: Not Free

LEGAL ENVIRONMENT: 21
POLITICAL INFLUENCES: 32
ECONOMIC PRESSURES: 23
TOTAL SCORE: 76

Although the transitional constitution provides for freedom of expression, the 1997 press law authorizes prepublication censorship and forbids the dissemination of "information inciting civil disobedience or serving as propaganda for enemies of the Burundian nation during a time of war." The state-run National Communication Council, which is charged with regulating the media, occasionally bans or suspends independent publications and restricts permissible reporting. In May, the media were barred from broadcasting interviews with rebel groups. In addition, reporters remain vulnerable to official harassment, detention, and violence, and many practice self-censorship. In March, police assaulted two journalists covering a demonstration and subjected one to arrest and questioning. The government owns and operates the main broadcast media as well as the country's only regularly published newspaper. Private publications and radio stations function sporadically, but some, such as Radio Publique Africaine, manage to present diverse and balanced views.

Cambodia

Status: Not Free

LEGAL ENVIRONMENT: 19
POLITICAL INFLUENCES: 21
ECONOMIC PRESSURES: 24
TOTAL SCORE: 64

The constitution provides for freedom of the press, and the present government publicly professes to support this right. While the press law provides journalists with several safeguards, it also permits the Information Ministry to suspend newspapers, broadly prohibits publishing articles that affect national security and political stability, and subjects the press to criminal statutes. During the year, authorities threatened a newspaper with suspension and detained several journalists. Moreover, the month-long suspensions of several papers in recent years continued to have a sobering effect on reporters. In December, a reporter was ambushed and beaten with an iron club by unidentified attackers, possibly in retaliation for a story regarding a land dispute. The private press routinely scrutinizes government policies and senior officials. However, the majority of broadcast media are controlled by the state both economically and editorially, according to a report by the World Press Freedom Committee, and programming favors the ruling party. The Information Ministry has denied repeated requests from opposition leader Sam Rainsy for a license to operate a radio station.

Cameroon

Status: Not Free

LEGAL ENVIRONMENT: 25
POLITICAL INFLUENCES: 22
ECONOMIC PRESSURES: 18
TOTAL SCORE: 65

The constitution provides for freedom of the press, but the penal code specifies that defamation, contempt, and dissemination of false news are punishable by prison terms and harsh fines, and the regime frequently uses libel laws to silence the independent print media. Nevertheless, at least 20 private newspapers publish regularly and are critical of the government. Ten years after the National Assembly passed a bill liberalizing the broadcast media, President Paul Biya signed the legislation into force in 2001. Despite prohibitive licensing fees, a number of private radio stations have applied for a license, while others continue to broadcast illegally. Coverage on the state-run media favors the ruling party, and reporters working at these news outlets have been punished for criticizing government policies. Although direct repression of the independent press eased somewhat during the year, journalists continued to be subject to some official harassment as well as arbitrary arrest and detention.

Canada
Status: Free

LEGAL ENVIRONMENT: 2
POLITICAL INFLUENCES: 7
ECONOMIC PRESSURES: 8
TOTAL SCORE: 17

A slightly diminished rating in 2002 is attributed more to problems arising from the concentration of ownership of the news media than from security restrictions such as the provisions of Bill 36, the anti-terrorism legislation that permits the increased surveillance of citizens. Both issues, however, are substantial challenges to press freedom. Censorship of editors and repression of dissenting views were attributed to CanWest Global Communications, the major media conglomerate. A newspaper publisher in the chain was sacked for printing an editorial critical of Prime Minister Jean Chretien. Responding to a pattern of such incidents, the national journalists association took the unusual step of seeking a parliamentary inquiry into the restrictions attributed to the owners of the newspaper group. A judicial gag order barred journalists from attending the preliminary hearing of an accused serial killer, even though such hearings are normally open to the press. The Toronto police used a warrant to seize raw television coverage in an investment fraud case. In March, a local school board threatened to withhold advertising from newspapers or broadcasters that the board felt had reported its affairs inaccurately.

Cape Verde

Status: Free

LEGAL ENVIRONMENT: 8
POLITICAL INFLUENCES: 11
ECONOMIC PRESSURES: 11
TOTAL SCORE: 30

Freedom of expression and of the press is guaranteed by law and generally respected in practice. Official authorization is not needed to publish newspapers, and there were no reports that the licensing system for broadcasters had been abused. Criminal libel laws remain on the books but have not recently been used to restrict news reporting. A growing independent press competes with state-owned broadcasters and newspapers. Journalists are free to scrutinize the government, but those at state-owned media outlets tend to practice self-censorship. Last year, the government exerted pressure on the media by suspending a newspaper and instituting management changes at the state television broadcaster.

Central African Republic

Status: Not Free

LEGAL ENVIRONMENT: 20
POLITICAL INFLUENCES: 28
ECONOMIC PRESSURES: 19
TOTAL SCORE: 67

Continuing political unrest during the year negatively affected access to information as well as journalists' ability to report the news freely. Legislation enacted in 1998 rescinded the government's authority to censor the press, but authorities have occasionally used criminal libel laws to prosecute journalists. Several independent newspapers publish sporadically and are critical of government policies and official corruption. However, broadcast media are dominated by the state and offer little coverage of opposition activities. Journalists remain subject to threats, violence, arbitrary arrest, and torture at the hands of the authorities. Reporters Sans Frontieres noted that after the attempted coup in October, the frequencies of two international radio stations were jammed, a French journalist was expelled from the country, and security forces threatened local journalists. In addition, a publisher was taken hostage by rebels for several weeks.

LEGAL ENVIRONMENT: 20
POLITICAL INFLUENCES: 26

Chad

ECONOMIC PRESSURES: 21

Status: Not Free

TOTAL SCORE: 67

Despite a constitutional provision for freedom of expression, the government restricts press freedom in practice. Libel is considered a criminal offense, and those convicted have received both prison sentences and fines. The media are subject to close official scrutiny and occasional censorship. A private radio station, FM Liberte, was suspended for three weeks in February after authorities accused it of broadcasting information "likely to disrupt public order." In April, authorities banned private radio stations from airing any political material prior to the parliamentary elections. The Union of Chadian Journalists issued a statement in November alleging that authorities at times refused reporters access to needed information sources and that correspondents were subjected to humiliating and debasing treatment while carrying out their job. A number of private newspapers circulate in the capital and are critical of government policies and leaders. However, radio remains the most important source of information, and state control over the majority of the broadcast media limits diverse or dissenting viewpoints. The only television station, Teletchad, is state-owned, and its coverage favors the government. Prohibitively high licensing fees for commercial radio stations limit new entrants into the market.

LEGAL ENVIRONMENT: 8
POLITICAL INFLUENCES: 8

Chile

ECONOMIC PRESSURES: 6

Status: Free

TOTAL SCORE: 22

The media maintain their independence, scrutinize the government, and cover issues sensitive to the military, including human rights. The Press Law passed in 2001 brought about sweeping reforms that rid the country of most criminal insult laws, protected journalists from the obligation to reveal their sources, and ended the power of the courts to issue gag laws on the press for reporting on controversial criminal cases. However, the law also limited the definition of a journalist to one who has graduated from a recognized journalism school. Despite the reforms, the penal code still prohibits insulting state institutions such as the presidency and the legislative and judicial bodies. In one case, the president of the Supreme Court brought charges against a businessman who, while participating in a talk show, insulted the courts by calling them immoral, cowardly, and corrupt. The man was briefly imprisoned but was released on bail and is awaiting trial. President Ricardo Lagos has put forward a bill that would eliminate all remaining insult laws on the books; however, the congress has yet to act on the legislation. In 2002, the media played a key role in fostering public awareness of the country's growing problem with public corruption. In another positive development, on October 30, the Senate approved a bill that will eliminate censorship of films.

	LEGAL ENVIRONMENT: 26
	POLITICAL INFLUENCES: 34
China	ECONOMIC PRESSURES: 20
Status: Not Free	TOTAL SCORE: 80

The government sharply restricts press freedom. A combination of statutes and directives forbid the media from promoting political reform, covering internal party politics or the inner workings of government, criticizing Beijing's domestic and international policies, or reporting financial data that the government has not released. All stories are potentially subject to prepublication censorship. However, authorities sometimes allow newspapers to report on corruption and other abuses by local officials. According to the Committee to Protect Journalists, as of December 2002 Chinese jails held 36 journalists, 14 of whom were serving time for publishing or distributing information online. Other journalists have been harassed, detained, threatened, or dismissed from their jobs because of their reporting. Officials also have suspended or shut down some liberal magazines, newspapers, and publishing houses. While China's print media are both public and private, the government owns and operates all radio and television stations. The government promotes use of the Internet, but regulates access, monitors use, and restricts and regulates content. A number of Internet cafes were closed during the year, and the government temporarily blocked all access to the Google and AltaVista search engines in September before backing down and focusing instead on preventing searches on sensitive topics. In Hong Kong, an unlikely combination of pro-democracy activists and businessmen criticized proposed national security legislation that they said could undermine the territory's traditionally free press and uninhibited flow of information.

Colombia

Status: Not Free

LEGAL ENVIRONMENT: 12
POLITICAL INFLUENCES: 32
ECONOMIC PRESSURES: 19

TOTAL SCORE: 63

Status change explanation: Colombia's rating changed from Partly Free to Not Free in order to reflect the worsening impact of the armed conflict on journalists.

Practicing journalism in the midst of the country's four-decades-old armed conflict is a hazardous profession. Although the press is vibrant and diverse, journalists have suffered enormous casualties in carrying out their duties. Legally, the constitution provides for press freedom, but laws to protect the press are not always enforced. Legislation introduced in 2002 and still under consideration would require journalists to obtain a certificate of suitability from the government and create a council to regulate journalists' work, while another bill would extend sanctions for libel. Journalists are frequently the targets of extrajudicial killings, violence, and harassment. During the year, there were several reports of kidnappings of journalists, threats that compelled some journalists to go into exile, and violent attacks on newspapers and television stations. The number of journalists murdered in Colombia is higher than in any other country in the world. According to the International Press Institute, at least 15 journalists were killed by leftist guerrillas, right-wing paramilitaries, drug traffickers, or common criminals in 2002. Some journalists refrain from publishing or broadcasting stories counter to the interests of these groups. Media concentration and general economic problems have led to more dependency on a smaller pool of advertisers, including the government, which the media often chose not to criticize.

Comoros

Status: Partly Free

LEGAL ENVIRONMENT: 9
POLITICAL INFLUENCES: 20
ECONOMIC PRESSURES: 14

TOTAL SCORE: 43

A new constitution adopted in December 2001 provides for freedom of speech and of the press, and these rights are generally respected. Nevertheless, journalists are occasionally sued for defamation. The semiofficial weekly *Al-Watwan* and several private newspapers are published regularly. Although the independent print and broadcast media operate without overt government interference and are critical of official policies, some journalists are believed to exercise self-censorship. A radio journalist arrested in November 2001 continued to be detained without charge during the year.

Congo, Republic of (Brazzaville)

Status: Partly Free

LEGAL ENVIRONMENT: 18
POLITICAL INFLUENCES: 20
ECONOMIC PRESSURES: 17
TOTAL SCORE: 55

The constitution adopted in January guarantees the basic right of press freedom, and the government generally respects this provision in practice. An August 2001 amendment to the 1996 press law abolished mandatory jail sentences for defamation, although it is still possible to face prison time in cases of "incitement to violence, racism and unrest," according to Reporters Sans Frontieres. About 10 private newspapers appear weekly in Brazzaville, and they often publish articles and editorials that are critical of the government. However, the government continues to monopolize the broadcast media, where coverage reflects official priorities and views. Reporters are occasionally subject to threats and intimidation at the hands of authorities. In July, a senior police official allegedly threatened a journalist during an interrogation session.

Congo, Democratic Republic of (Kinshasa)

Status: Not Free

LEGAL ENVIRONMENT: 25
POLITICAL INFLUENCES: 35
ECONOMIC PRESSURES: 22
TOTAL SCORE: 82

Statutes provide for freedom of the press, but the government continues to sharply restrict the work of journalists through a variety of means. The 1996 Press Law prescribes the death penalty for reporters convicted of disseminating false news, insulting the army, demoralizing the nation, or betraying the state in time of war. Harsh criminal libel laws were used to convict, jail, and fine several journalists during the year. The number of private newspapers and radio stations—many of which are associated with and financed by political parties, military factions, or the Roman Catholic church—is growing, but the state-controlled broadcasting network reaches the largest number of citizens. Meanwhile, in areas under the control of the various rebel factions, independent media barely exist. Reporters continue to face frequent threats and intimidation, physical attacks, and arrest and detention at the hands of authorities. Rebels and other groups also threaten and attack journalists. According to the local watchdog group Journaliste en Danger, 33 journalists were arrested in 2002. Of these, 9 were detained in rebel-held territories, and 24 in regions under the government's control. Some of those detained were allegedly tortured while in custody. Official harassment also includes the censoring of sensitive news broadcasts and the seizure of newspapers. The financial viability of media outlets remains hampered by high production costs as well as high mandatory registration fees and broadcasting taxes.

Costa Rica

Status: Free

LEGAL ENVIRONMENT: 4
POLITICAL INFLUENCES: 5
ECONOMIC PRESSURES: 5
TOTAL SCORE: 14

Costa Rica has highly diverse and independent media with a half dozen major, privately owned newspapers, several private television stations, and almost 100 privately run radio stations that present an array of opinions. Most significant in 2002 was the elimination of the country's "insult laws," which provided criminal penalties of up to three years in prison for insulting the honor of a public official. The move was highly welcomed; however, libel, slander, and defamation continue to be criminal offenses. In general, the media are free from political influence. There were no reports of harassment or intimidation, but the government remains under pressure to identify and punish those responsible for the 2001 murder of journalist Parmenio Medina. Private ownership of media outlets is somewhat concentrated.

Cote d'Ivoire

Status: Not Free

LEGAL ENVIRONMENT: 18
POLITICAL INFLUENCES: 33
ECONOMIC PRESSURES: 17
TOTAL SCORE: 68

Although the constitution provides for freedom of expression, this right is restricted in practice. The law allows the government to initiate criminal libel proceedings against persons who insult the president or prime minister, defame institutions of the state, or undermine the reputation of the nation. The National Press Commission is charged with enforcing regulations relating to the creation and ownership of the media. Dozens of independent newspapers, many of which have links to political parties, criticize official policies freely, while state-owned newspapers and a state-run broadcasting system are usually unreservedly pro-government. Press freedom suffered in 2002, as the media was caught in the midst of a protracted political crisis sparked by a military uprising in late September. Shortly after the crisis erupted, the government jammed the broadcasts of several foreign news broadcasters, accusing them of attempting to destabilize the country. A number of local and foreign journalists were assaulted by mobs or security forces, or were detained by the police. On September 21, supporters of the ruling party beat Mamadou Keita, a reporter for the opposition newspaper *Le Patriote*. A group of some 50 people ransacked and looted the offices of the private Mayama media group, publisher of three pro-opposition publications. Continuing threats and physical harassment led to increased self-censorship on the part of the media by the end of the year.

Croatia

Status: Partly Free

LEGAL ENVIRONMENT: 8
POLITICAL INFLUENCES: 12
ECONOMIC PRESSURES: 13
TOTAL SCORE: 33

While the government has substantially expanded the boundaries of press freedom in recent years, the events of 2002 demonstrated mixed progress. Article 38 of the constitution bans censorship and guarantees freedom of expression and the press. Nevertheless, in February, authorities prohibited the broadcast of a televised debate on judicial corruption. State officials claimed that the discussion amounted to coercion of the courts, and threatened the host with criminal prosecution. Also during the year, a Zagreb court levied heavy libel fines against the satirical weekly *Feral Tribune* for articles published during the regime of former president Franjo Tudjman. Later in the year, a judge dismissed a libel suit brought by Tudjman's widow against five editors at Croatian State Television (HRT). The station had previously aired a documentary implicating President Tudjman in war crimes. HRT became a public service broadcaster in 2001. International organizations, such as the OSCE, have expressed concern that the HRT's change in status leaves open the opportunity for political influence on the broadcaster's governing board.

Cuba

Status: Not Free

LEGAL ENVIRONMENT: 30
POLITICAL INFLUENCES: 36
ECONOMIC PRESSURES: 28
TOTAL SCORE: 94

In 2002, the situation for the press remained grim in Cuba, the only country in the Western Hemisphere that systematically imprisons journalists for their work. It is illegal for journalists to express opinions contrary to those of the state, and laws against criticizing the government, the revolution, and its leaders are punishable by jail time. The government controls all media outlets in the country including the main daily newspaper *Granma,* which serves as an official mouthpiece. Electronic media are also controlled by the state, and access to foreign media is restricted. Of the estimated 100 independent journalists operating in the country, many are regularly harassed, beaten, detained, or imprisoned by state officials. However, one notable event in 2002 stemmed from the visit of former U.S. president Jimmy Carter to Cuba, where he delivered an unprecedented and uncensored live speech on Cuban television. Also during the year, the government prohibited the sale of personal computers to the general public in order to prevent the emergence of independent publications and to keep the Internet age further at bay. All media are dependent on the state both for funding and for the right to operate.

Cyprus

Status: Free

LEGAL ENVIRONMENT: 4
POLITICAL INFLUENCES: 6
ECONOMIC PRESSURES: 8
TOTAL SCORE: 18

Freedom of the press is generally respected in law and practice in the Greek area. A vibrant independent press frequently criticizes authorities, and private television and radio stations in the Greek Cypriot community compete effectively with government-controlled stations. In April 2002, the Greek Cypriot attorney general demanded that television stations surrender videotape of a public demonstration. Critics charged that the demand threatened a journalist's right to protect sources. In the disputed north, Turkish Cypriot authorities are overtly hostile to the independent press. In late 2001, a Turkish Cypriot court forced the closure of the main opposition paper *Avrupa*. During 2002, authorities imprisoned two editors from the paper's successor, *Afrika*, for criticizing the Turkish Cypriot leader. [The numerical rating for Cyprus is based on the situation in the Greek side of the island.]

Czech Republic
Status: Free

LEGAL ENVIRONMENT: 9
POLITICAL INFLUENCES: 5
ECONOMIC PRESSURES: 9
TOTAL SCORE: 23

The government respects freedom of expression and of the press. The charter of rights prohibits speech against individual rights, public security, public health, and morality. However, libel remains a criminal offense and journalists face prison terms if convicted. The controversial lawsuit against the weekly newspaper *Respekt* drew to a close in April, when judicial authorities ordered the publication to apologize for publishing vague allegations of corruption against a government official. Later in the year, law enforcement officials were quick to foil an alleged plot to assassinate an investigative journalist. In 2001, parliament passed a bill designed to limit political influence over state-controlled Czech Television. Under the law, nongovernmental groups, rather than politicians, will nominate members to the organization's governing council. A 2002 law applies a similar system to Czech Radio. Currently, there are three national television stations (one public and two private) and approximately 60 private radio stations.

Denmark
Status: Free

LEGAL ENVIRONMENT: 1
POLITICAL INFLUENCES: 3
ECONOMIC PRESSURES: 7
TOTAL SCORE: 11

The media enjoy strong constitutional protections for free expression and a long tradition of press freedom. Independent print and broadcast media represent a wide variety of views and are frequently critical of the government. In August, however, reports surfaced that police had secretly recorded telephone conversations between journalist Stig Matthiesen and an editor at the newspaper *Jyllands-Posten*. Matthiesen was preparing a story on an alleged Muslim "death list" containing the names of prominent Danish Jews. He subsequently refused to cooperate with a court order to reveal his sources. The government provides subsidies to radio and television broadcasters. Although state-owned TV companies maintain independent editorial boards, private radio stations are tightly regulated.

Djibouti

Status: Not Free

LEGAL ENVIRONMENT: 21
POLITICAL INFLUENCES: 25
ECONOMIC PRESSURES: 19
TOTAL SCORE: 65

Despite constitutional protection, the government often restricts freedom of speech. Slander is prohibited, and other laws that prohibit the dissemination of "false information" and regulate the publication of newspapers have been used against the independent press. Although private publications are generally allowed to circulate freely and provide some criticism of official policies, many journalists exercise self-censorship. The state owns and closely controls all electronic media as well as the country's principal newspaper, *La Nation*, and coverage favors the government. Djibouti and the United States in 2002 agreed to set up radio relay stations in Djibouti to broadcast Arabic radio programs of the Voice of America.

Dominica

Status: Free

LEGAL ENVIRONMENT: 0
POLITICAL INFLUENCES: 6
ECONOMIC PRESSURES: 8
TOTAL SCORE: 14

The press is free, diverse, and critical and offers a variety of viewpoints. There are no laws that constrain press freedom. A few private newspapers as well as political party journals constitute the print media. The broadcast media consist of one independent radio station and one state-owned radio station. Although, in general, media outlets operate freely without government interference, the state-owned radio station operates under a government-appointed board that exerts some political influence over content and editorial stances.

Dominican Republic

Status: Partly Free

LEGAL ENVIRONMENT: 5
POLITICAL INFLUENCES: 10
ECONOMIC PRESSURES: 18
TOTAL SCORE: 33

Status change explanation: The Dominican Republic's rating moved from Free to Partly Free as a result of increased economic pressures on media outlets.

Press freedom is generally respected and is provided for in the constitution. However, political and economic pressures increased on the media during the year. There is an abundance of privately owned media outlets, including several daily and weekly newspapers as well as numerous radio and television stations, that offer a wide array of coverage. President Hipolito Mejia continues to have a confrontational attitude toward journalists who criticize his administration. Journalists practice self-censorship when their reporting has the possibility of affecting government officials' and media owners' political or economic interests. In one instance, the news director of Radio Marien was arrested for having reported on rice trafficking on the border with Haiti, a sensitive issue for government authorities. In addition, it is generally believed that some major media outlets refrain from serious and sustained reporting of police misconduct, particularly in the case of excessive use of force and extrajudicial killings, in order not to hurt the island republic's key tourism industry. Media ownership is concentrated in the hands of a few elites, which affects the diversity of content. The state exerts economic pressure on the media through denial of advertising revenues and imposition of taxes on imported newsprint. Many journalists have complained about the economic situation, which includes low wages that induce some to accept bribes.

East Timor

Status: Free

LEGAL ENVIRONMENT: 3
POLITICAL INFLUENCES: 8
ECONOMIC PRESSURES: 11
TOTAL SCORE: 22

The new constitution adopted in March protects freedom of expression, but also allows the government to suspend rights in cases affecting national security or in order to protect "human dignity." State-run public radio and television services began operating when the country achieved full independence in May, replacing the broadcasting media operated by the interim UN administration. Like other services run by the cash-strapped government, however, the new broadcasting system faced problems, with Radio East Timor at times unavailable in parts of the country because of power shortages. Two independent dailies and a number of weekly publications cover a diverse range of views. While there are no legal impediments to establishing new media, entrants into the market are constrained by insufficient financial resources. In November, authorities indicted two Indonesian military officers for the 1999 killing of Dutch journalist Sander Thoenes.

Ecuador

Status: Partly Free

LEGAL ENVIRONMENT: 14
POLITICAL INFLUENCES: 14
ECONOMIC PRESSURES: 13
TOTAL SCORE: 41

The constitution provides for freedom of the press, but laws that prevent the exercise of this freedom remain on the books. Four articles in the criminal code penalize defamation of the president, court officials, or corporate heads, although charges are rarely brought against journalists under these laws. Journalists practice some self-censorship regarding sensitive political topics or stories about the military. In addition, media owners, some of whom have narrow regional economic interests, frequently set journalists' agendas and editorial stances. Most media outlets in the country are privately owned.

Egypt

Status: Not Free

LEGAL ENVIRONMENT: 28
POLITICAL INFLUENCES: 27
ECONOMIC PRESSURES: 24
TOTAL SCORE: 79

Vaguely worded statutes in the Press Law, the Publications Law, the penal code, and libel laws restrict press freedom. Direct criticism of the president, his family, or the military, as well as criticism of foreign heads of state, can result in imprisonment and the closure of publications. The government owns and operates most television and radio stations. However, control over the broadcast media was slightly diminished this year as Al-Mihwar, the country's first independent television channel, began broadcasting. Three major dailies are owned in part by the state, and the president appoints their editor. The Internet is widely available, and the government does not significantly monitor or censor content. Although there are a number of privately owned print media outlets, the government exercises indirect control over them through its monopoly on printing and distribution.

El Salvador
Status: Partly Free

LEGAL ENVIRONMENT: 9
POLITICAL INFLUENCES: 18
ECONOMIC PRESSURES: 11
TOTAL SCORE: 38

The media are privately owned and pluralistic, and media outlets freely scrutinize the government and report on opposition activities. However, there are several laws that constrain press freedom. Article 24 of the Law of National Defense requires journalists to reveal their sources if the "national interest" is at stake. Article 46 of the Enabling Law of the State Audit Court allows the court to keep secret its audits of government officials handling taxpayers' money, which could impede journalists' ability to investigate corruption and to hold officials accountable. On May 1, opposition leader Shafik Handal called journalists liars and said the media should not be trusted. The statements incited his supporters to insult and physically attack journalists who were present at the time. Some media outlets have complained that official advertising often favors the pro-government media, which in some circumstances encourages journalists to practice self-censorship.

Equatorial Guinea
Status: Not Free

LEGAL ENVIRONMENT: 26
POLITICAL INFLUENCES: 32
ECONOMIC PRESSURES: 23
TOTAL SCORE: 81

Press freedom is constitutionally guaranteed, but the government tightly restricts this right in practice. All journalists are required to register with the Information Ministry, and in May strict accreditation procedures for all foreign correspondents were introduced. The 1992 press law authorizes government censorship of all publications. While mild criticism of public institutions is allowed, disparaging comments about the president or security forces are not tolerated and self-censorship is commonplace. In July, opposition leader Fabian Nseu Guema was sentenced to one year in prison and fined $45,000 for insulting the president on the Internet. A few small, independent newspapers publish sporadically, but nearly all print and broadcast media are state-run and tightly controlled. Although foreign publications have become more widely available in recent years, several journalists, political leaders, and association heads complained in 2002 of increasing difficulties in accessing the Internet. Police verbally threatened independent reporters covering the trial of opposition figures in May, and several were barred from the courtroom. The local journalists' association has been subjected to repeated harassment and closure, and in July its head, Pedro Nolasco Ndong, fled the country after receiving threats related to his reporting.

Eritrea

Status: Not Free

LEGAL ENVIRONMENT: 26
POLITICAL INFLUENCES: 36
ECONOMIC PRESSURES: 21
TOTAL SCORE: 83

Conditions for the media continued to be severely constrained in 2002. Although freedom of expression is nominally provided for in the constitution, the 1996 press law makes this right subject to the official interpretation of "the objective reality of Eritrea," forbids private ownership of the broadcast media, and requires that all newspapers and reporters be licensed. In September 2001, in a dramatic crackdown against the independent media and other forms of political dissent, the government banned all privately owned newspapers and arrested at least 10 leading journalists, ostensibly on the grounds of national security. The arrests of other members of the press during 2002 brought the total number of imprisoned journalists to 18, according to the Committee to Protect Journalists. After some of the detainees began a hunger strike in April, they were transferred from prison to unknown places of detention and held incommunicado. At least six journalists have fled abroad, while most foreign correspondents have also left Eritrea as they are unable to operate freely.

LEGAL ENVIRONMENT: 7
POLITICAL INFLUENCES: 4

Estonia
ECONOMIC PRESSURES: 6

Status: Free
TOTAL SCORE: 17

Estonia maintains one of the most open press environments of all the former Soviet republics. Article 45 of the constitution bans censorship and guarantees freedom of expression. Local journalists enjoy these rights in practice. A variety of independent dailies publish in the Estonian and Russian languages, although existing legislation compels the use of Estonian on all signs, advertisements, and public notices. Defamation remains a criminal offense; however, there were no reported cases during the year. A relatively large number of media organizations compete for limited market share and advertising revenue. As a result, many media outlets are in financial trouble. The government provides subsidies to the state television broadcaster and likewise maintains formal ownership of the central printing house. Publication and distribution are generally free from political influence.

LEGAL ENVIRONMENT: 23
POLITICAL INFLUENCES: 23

Ethiopia
ECONOMIC PRESSURES: 18

Status: Not Free
TOTAL SCORE: 64

A 1992 law guarantees freedom of the press, but also forbids publishing articles that are defamatory, threaten the safety of the state, agitate for war, or incite ethnic conflict. Throughout the year, harsh criminal libel laws were used to prosecute and fine or jail a number of journalists, including the head of the Ethiopian Free Press Journalists' Association (EFJA). At least several dozen more journalists have fled the country and live in self-imposed exile rather than face pending court cases. In July and August, international press freedom advocates as well as the EFJA expressed concern over the government's plan to introduce a new press law and a code of ethics, which they feared could be used to further restrict the operations of the media. Although legal action continues to be the most prevalent form of official harassment, reporters are also subjected to occasional intimidation and physical violence at the hands of police and security forces. Broadcast media are largely state-run, and some journalists practice self-censorship. The independent print media remain lively and critical of the government, but most publications are not distributed widely throughout the country. High annual licensing fees and bureaucratic licensing procedures impose additional restraints on newspapers' ability to publish, while reporters continue to have trouble gaining access to official information.

Fiji

Status: Free

LEGAL ENVIRONMENT: 6
POLITICAL INFLUENCES: 11
ECONOMIC PRESSURES: 12
TOTAL SCORE: 29

Status change explanation: Fiji's rating improved from Partly Free to Free to reflect greater political stability and the increased ability of the media to operate freely.

Press freedom is generally respected, although legal constraints on the media remain on the books. Newspapers are required to register with the government in order to publish. Though it has never been used, the Press Correction Act authorizes officials to arrest anyone who publishes "malicious" material, or to demand a "correcting statement" for an allegedly false or distorted article. Provisions in the 1998 Emergency Powers Act allow parliament to restrict civil liberties, including press freedom, during a state of emergency. Private media outlets report on alleged official wrongdoing, but some self-censorship persists. The government owns shares in the *Fiji Post* newspaper and has business links to its main competitor, the *Fiji Sun*, which raises questions about the concentration of media ownership and independence. Authorities have at times pressured editors and otherwise interfered with the press. During the year, officials subjected the press to verbal attacks, and police raided a journalist's home in April after he refused to hand over confidential documents.

Finland

Status: Free

LEGAL ENVIRONMENT: 1
POLITICAL INFLUENCES: 2
ECONOMIC PRESSURES: 7
TOTAL SCORE: 10

The government respects freedom of the press and guarantees the right of reply in cases of slander. The country supports more than 200 newspapers. Although most are in private hands, some have connections to political parties or their affiliates. With the exception of two public service channels, all radio and television broadcasters are privately operated. Internet access is open and unrestricted. Per capita Internet use is among the highest in the world.

France

Status: Free

LEGAL ENVIRONMENT: 5
POLITICAL INFLUENCES: 7
ECONOMIC PRESSURES: 5
TOTAL SCORE: 17

The constitution and governing institutions maintain a free and open press environment. More than 100 daily newspapers offer a variety of perspectives, and most print publications are privately owned. Critics warn that the courts have begun to rule against journalists in cases of libel and the protection of confidential sources. During the past two years, law enforcement officials have detained five journalists in order to compel them to reveal sources in criminal investigations. Satellite and cable television has grown substantially in recent years. Commercial radio continues to hold a large audience. Internet access is open and unrestricted.

Gabon

Status: Partly Free

LEGAL ENVIRONMENT: 20
POLITICAL INFLUENCES: 20
ECONOMIC PRESSURES: 18
TOTAL SCORE: 58

The government sometimes restricts freedom of expression in spite of a constitutional provision that press freedom be respected. The communications code specifies the responsibilities as well as the rights of journalists. The state is authorized by law to initiate criminal libel proceedings against those who defame elected government officials and is also permitted to criminalize civil libel suits. The National Communications Council (CNC), a government agency charged with upholding journalistic standards, regularly suspends the publication or broadcasting licenses of media outlets. In September, the CNC banned two independent weeklies for three months after they published reports on alleged official corruption. The government owns the only daily newspaper as well as the majority of broadcast media outlets. At least 10 private publications, some of which are controlled by opposition political parties, publish irregularly, while financial considerations limit the viability of the independent broadcast media. International press freedom advocates have reported that President Omar Bongo uses state subsidies to reward pro-government independent media outlets and that some journalists are susceptible to bribery.

The Gambia

Status: Not Free

LEGAL ENVIRONMENT: 20
POLITICAL INFLUENCES: 27
ECONOMIC PRESSURES: 18
TOTAL SCORE: 65

The government significantly restricts free expression even though this right is provided for in the constitution. Several decrees require all private media to pay large licensing fees in order to operate. International press freedom organizations protested the passing of a restrictive media bill by the National Assembly. The National Media Commission Bill, which President Yahya Jammeh had not yet signed into law by the end of 2002, would give government authorities the power to license journalists, to deny the right to confidentiality of sources, to formulate a journalistic code of ethics, and to punish the media for noncompliance. Despite some self-censorship and a lack of access to official information, the independent media continue to criticize government policies as well as the ruling party. However, the state-run broadcast media present tightly controlled news and give limited coverage to opposition viewpoints. Journalists and media outlets are subject to intimidation and harassment at the hands of police and other authorities. During the year, at least two reporters were detained, held without charge, and questioned by the secret service.

Georgia

Status: Partly Free

LEGAL ENVIRONMENT: 18
POLITICAL INFLUENCES: 21
ECONOMIC PRESSURES: 15
TOTAL SCORE: 54

The independent media struggle in the face of continued political and economic pressure. Article 24 of the constitution bans censorship and provides for freedom of expression. The 1991 Law on the Press and

Other Mass Media allows for a wide degree of press freedom; however, the law lacks effective enforcement mechanisms. To address weaknesses in existing legislation, parliament introduced the Law on Freedom of Speech and Media during 2002. Local nongovernmental organizations and civic groups generally applauded the measure but raised concerns that sections regarding media registration and national security could potentially restrict reporting. The bill passed on its first reading but had not entered into force by the end of the year. The 1999 administrative code provides for open access to public information. Adherence to this regulation varies widely. The limited space for press freedom diminishes rapidly outside the capital of Tbilisi. In June, the Bolnisi town mayor physically assaulted a female journalist after she reported on election irregularities in a recent local election. In September, law enforcement agents damaged equipment and assaulted the staff of a Zugdidi television station after the channel broadcast a story on police corruption. The great majority of print and broadcast outlets are privately owned; however, the state continues to maintain control over the only nationwide television and radio stations. Private media have demonstrated marked dependence on powerful economic or political interests.

Germany

Status: Free

LEGAL ENVIRONMENT: 2
POLITICAL INFLUENCES: 6
ECONOMIC PRESSURES: 7
TOTAL SCORE: 15

Article 5 of the German basic law guarantees freedom of expression and of the press. German media largely enjoy these rights in practice, although existing legislation creates exceptions for hate speech, Holocaust denial, and Nazi propaganda. The 1997 Teleservices Law prohibits Internet access to obscene, violent, or "dangerous" material. Local and regional dailies are the most common types of newspapers and present the image of a pluralistic press. Yet, in the past two decades, financial pressures have consolidated the private media sector to the point where a handful of centralized editorial offices produce most of the content. In fact, a few large corporations, such as Axel Springer Verlag and Bertelsmann, control a sizable share of all print and broadcast outlets. The states (Lander) generally oversee public radio and television broadcasters. These public media outlets draw their primary funding from licensing fees.

Legal environment: 7
Political influences: 11

Ghana

Economic pressures: 12

Status: Free

Total Score: 30

Freedom of expression is constitutionally guaranteed and generally respected. Fulfilling a campaign promise, the government of President John Kufuor in 2001 repealed Ghana's criminal libel and sedition laws and otherwise eased pressure on the press. However, the 1994 Emergency Powers Act allows the government to censor news from disturbed areas. In March, officials imposed prepublication censorship on stories about an outbreak of interclan violence in the north of the country. The National Media Commission, an independent government body, is responsible for monitoring the media and maintaining journalistic standards. While major government media outlets exercise some restraint in their coverage, they do report on allegations of official corruption and mismanagement. In addition, several private newspapers freely criticize the administration. However, in August, an editor in chief received death threats from alleged supporters of the former president. Poorly paid journalists are reportedly susceptible to bribery.

Legal environment: 14
Political influences: 6

Greece

Economic pressures: 8

Status: Free

Total Score: 28

Article 14 of the constitution bans censorship and guarantees freedom of expression. While the government has at times acted to restrict press freedom, Greek media generally enjoy these rights in practice. Libel of and insults against the president remain criminal offenses and carry the threat of fines or imprisonment. In 2001, an ethnic minority activist was fined and sentenced to prison for allegedly distributing false information. There were no reported criminal libel cases against journalists in 2002. Until recently, the broadcast sector, particularly radio, existed largely without regulation. Then, in 2001, the government sparked a notable public backlash when it attempted to license the country's estimated 1,700 unregulated broadcasters. The government did, however, allow broadcasters to operate throughout the licensing process. The majority of newspapers are privately owned. Some journalists experienced harassment and assault while covering the arrests of members of the November 17 terrorist group.

Grenada

Status: Free

LEGAL ENVIRONMENT: 5
POLITICAL INFLUENCES: 3
ECONOMIC PRESSURES: 6
TOTAL SCORE: 14

Grenada continues to enjoy a free press, which is guaranteed by the constitution. A privately owned corporation, with a minority government share, owns the principal radio and television stations; additional outlets are privately owned. Both print and broadcast media outlets operate freely without state intervention and present a wide variety of views including those of the opposition. Reporters, however, operate cautiously under slander and libel laws, which the state commonly uses to prosecute journalists. In one case, the editor of the weekly newspaper *Grenada Today* is facing charges of defamatory libel for an article that was critical of the government. After two years on the run in Canada, a prominent journalist, accused of sedition on the basis of statements made during a radio show in 1998, surrendered to authorities.

Guatemala

Status: Partly Free

LEGAL ENVIRONMENT: 16
POLITICAL INFLUENCES: 30
ECONOMIC PRESSURES: 12
TOTAL SCORE: 58

Press freedom is enshrined in Guatemala's constitution, and newspapers freely scrutinize government policies. However, laws to protect journalists are rarely enforced and legislation passed in 2001 requires that all journalists be licensed. During 2002, there were numerous cases of members of the press being targets of threats, harassment, and intimidation. Reporters who expose corruption or investigate past human rights abuses stemming from the country's civil war are particularly vulnerable. Consequently, many journalists are inclined to practice self-censorship. All four of the country's television stations are owned by a Mexican citizen and have been criticized for being monopolistic and pro-government, and for reporting only on uncontroversial issues. The government places high costs on the establishment of radio stations through public auctioning of frequencies. In a country with a majority indigenous population, this practice creates an effective barrier to rural indigenous communities gaining access to or control of media outlets.

Guinea

Status: Not Free

LEGAL ENVIRONMENT: 25
POLITICAL INFLUENCES: 30
ECONOMIC PRESSURES: 19
TOTAL SCORE: 74

Despite a constitutional provision for freedom of expression, the press is subject to a considerable number of legal restrictions. The government has wide powers to bar any communications that insult the president or disturb the peace. In addition, defamation and slander are considered criminal offenses. In 2001, two journalists were imprisoned after being charged with defamation. All broadcasting outlets, as well as the country's only daily newspaper, are state-controlled and avoid politically sensitive stories. However, a number of independent publications in Conakry, the capital, offer sharp criticism of the government despite frequent harassment. Several journalists were arbitrarily arrested during the year as a result of their reporting. High printing costs hamper the expansion of the private media.

Guinea-Bissau

Status: Partly Free

LEGAL ENVIRONMENT: 15
POLITICAL INFLUENCES: 27
ECONOMIC PRESSURES: 18
TOTAL SCORE: 60

Although freedom of speech and of the press is constitutionally guaranteed, the government imposes some limitations on the press. Officials encourage journalists to practice self-censorship, and reporters are also subjected to occasional harassment and arbitrary arrest. The editor of the independent daily *Correio de Bissau* was detained for two days in June and was accused of criticizing President Kumba Yala on the private radio station Radio Bombolom. In December, a Portuguese television station was barred from broadcasting for an unspecified period. However, two private newspapers that had been indefinitely closed in late 2001 on the grounds that they threatened national security were allowed to resume publishing in 2002. The state-run print and broadcast media rarely question or criticize government policies. Few private newspapers publish regularly, largely because of financial constraints and their dependence on the state-owned printing press.

Guyana

Status: Free

LEGAL ENVIRONMENT: 5
POLITICAL INFLUENCES: 5
ECONOMIC PRESSURES: 11
TOTAL SCORE: 21

The constitution provides for press freedom, and the government generally respects this right in practice. There is one major independent daily newspaper, the *Stabroek News*, and one government daily newspaper, the *Guyana Chronicle*. While in the past the government operated the country's only radio station, the government has responded to criticism that it controls the electronic media by granting new radio operating licenses. In addition to one state-run television station, there are a dozen independent stations throughout the country.

Haiti

Status: Not Free

LEGAL ENVIRONMENT: 17
POLITICAL INFLUENCES: 39
ECONOMIC PRESSURES: 23
TOTAL SCORE: 79

Although press freedom is provided for in the constitution, laws to protect the press are rarely enforced. Moreover, government respect for press freedom deteriorated in the past year. The reach of the print media is severely limited by the high rate of illiteracy in the country. Broadcast media, on the other hand, are plentiful, with several hundred radio stations operating throughout Haiti. Journalists are frequently harassed by government supporters and are sometimes subjected to physical violence. Although journalists are critical of the government, investigative journalism is rare and many journalists practice self-censorship. Those responsible for the December 2001 hacking to death of journalist Brignol Lindor and the April 2000 murder of journalist Jean Leopold Dominique have not yet been brought to justice. Attacks on the press increased toward the end of the year in the wake of antigovernment protests in the north; one radio station was partially torched, and several journalists were forced into hiding after receiving threats from a pro-Aristide militia known as the "Cannibal Army." Many radio stations reportedly censor content so as not to lose advertising funds. Because of the extremely poor economic situation in Haiti, journalists can be susceptible to bribery.

Honduras

LEGAL ENVIRONMENT: 16
POLITICAL INFLUENCES: 19
ECONOMIC PRESSURES: 16

Status: Partly Free

TOTAL SCORE: 51

Although the constitution provides for freedom of the press, there are several laws that constrain this right. Laws that prohibit defamation and require journalists to reveal their sources in special circumstances are on the books. In addition, journalists are required to be licensed under the 1972 Organic Law of the College of Journalists. In 2001 the Inter-American Commission on Human Rights reported that the government had impeded public scrutiny of its actions. The line between politics and the media is obscured, as a number of the major media outlets are owned and operated by powerful politicians who frequently set editorial policy and decide on coverage. Some journalists have admitted to self-censorship in order to avoid offending media owners' political and economic interests. There were several reports of harassment of journalists reporting on official corruption. Nongovernmental ownership of media outlets is extremely concentrated in the hands of a small, powerful business elite. Independent media have complained of discrimination in the placement of official government advertising.

Hungary

LEGAL ENVIRONMENT: 4
POLITICAL INFLUENCES: 10
ECONOMIC PRESSURES: 9

Status: Free

TOTAL SCORE: 23

Independent media thrive, but some political interference continues to trouble the press. Article 61 of the constitution provides for freedom of expression and the press. A 1996 media law requires both ruling and opposition parties to share appointments to state media oversight boards.

Opposition parties had accused the previous government of stacking the oversight boards. After losing power in 2002, the former ruling party accused the new government of improperly influencing state television and radio. The main opposition newspaper, *Magyar Nemzet*, alleged that the new government was exerting inappropriate pressure on its advertisers, thus endangering the paper's financial viability. Pro-government media outlets at times receive better access to official information. Hungary's two national private television broadcasters attract the vast majority of country's viewers, while the three state-owned stations account for roughly 10 percent. Numerous private radio stations operate throughout Hungary. All of the country's national newspapers are privately owned.

Iceland
Status: Free

LEGAL ENVIRONMENT: 1
POLITICAL INFLUENCES: 2
ECONOMIC PRESSURES: 5
TOTAL SCORE: 8

Iceland has an exceptionally open and free media environment. The constitution and governing institutions provide strong guarantees of freedom of expression. Current legislation, however, restricts the production and distribution of films depicting violence against people or animals. In the past six years, the state Motion Picture Review Committee has censored more than 20 films for being unsuitable for children. Independent and party-affiliated newspapers offer a variety of perspectives. The country maintains a mixture of both private and public television stations. An autonomous board of directors oversees the state broadcasting service. Internet access is open and unrestricted. More than 80 percent of the population access the Internet from their homes.

India
Status: Partly Free

LEGAL ENVIRONMENT: 13
POLITICAL INFLUENCES: 20
ECONOMIC PRESSURES: 12
TOTAL SCORE: 45

The private press is vigorous although journalists continue to face a number of constraints. In recent years, the government has occasionally used its power under the Official Secrets Act (OSA) to restrict the publication of sensitive stories. In June, Kashmiri reporter Iftikhar Ali Gilani was arrested, charged under the OSA, and detained for more than seven months before the military admitted that the case against him was baseless. Intimidation of journalists by a variety of actors increased in 2002 and led to some self-censorship, particularly among the regional media. Three reporters were killed during the year, police attacked journalists covering a peace demonstration in Gujarat in April, and an attack on a Tamil Nadu–based newspaper in July left several journalists injured. The *New York Times* reported that in the troubled state of Jammu and Kashmir, four journalists were shot at and wounded by separatist militants between April and September. Official harassment of the investigative Internet news portal Tehelka.com and one of its funders continued during the year. Radio is both public and private, but the state-owned All India Radio enjoys a dominant position and its news coverage favors the government. Television is no longer a government monopoly; according to the government press agency, 90 percent of channels are privately owned. In June, the government ended a 50-year ban on foreign ownership of the print media.

Indonesia

Status: Partly Free

LEGAL ENVIRONMENT: 19
POLITICAL INFLUENCES: 25
ECONOMIC PRESSURES: 12
TOTAL SCORE: 56

While the constitution contains a general provision for freedom of expression, the Indonesian media remain constrained by growing legal restrictions, as well as by continuing threats and violence directed at journalists. Local and international groups expressed concern about a new broadcasting bill passed at the end of November. The bill creates a national broadcasting commission, chosen by parliament and answerable to the president, that is responsible for monitoring news content and has the power to shut down or otherwise penalize media outlets that contravene the law. The private press, freed from its Suharto-era shackles, generally reports aggressively on government policies, corruption, political protests, civil conflict, and other formerly taboo issues. However, some journalists practice self-censorship, and poorly paid reporters remain susceptible to bribery. Most private broadcast media still are owned or have management ties to the family of former president Suharto.

According to the Alliance of Indonesian Journalists (AJI), the intimidation of journalists by police, the security forces, extremist religious groups, and separatist rebels, particularly in the outlying provinces, remains a serious problem. Throughout the year, AJI recorded a number of cases of violent attacks on reporters by police officers and other assailants. Foreign correspondents require special visas to enter the country and are barred from traveling to conflict areas. In March, authorities refused to renew the visa of Australian reporter Lindsay Murdoch, probably as a result of his critical reporting.

Iran
Status: Not Free

LEGAL ENVIRONMENT: 25
POLITICAL INFLUENCES: 32
ECONOMIC PRESSURES: 19
TOTAL SCORE: 76

Freedom of the press and of expression continued to be a central issue between hard-liners and political reformers in the country. The media are vibrant and critical despite official attempts to limit press freedom. Journalists are subjected to harsh prison sentences and exorbitant fines and even the death penalty for violating vaguely worded laws that prohibit insulting Islam, or criticizing the Islamic Revolution and its supreme leader. Self-censorship is widely practiced as a result. The country's conservative Press Court sentenced dozens of journalists, mostly pro-reformists, to prison during the year. Iran has the highest number of imprisoned journalists in the Middle East. More than 80 publications have been shut down in the country since a crackdown on the independent press began in April 2000. A commission dominated by religious hard-liners was recently established to monitor the Internet and news Web sites considered to be "illegal."

Iraq
Status: Not Free

LEGAL ENVIRONMENT: 29
POLITICAL INFLUENCES: 39
ECONOMIC PRESSURES: 27
TOTAL SCORE: 95

Revolutionary Command Council decrees and the penal code do not allow anything to be published that is not in strict accordance to the views of the ruling Ba'ath Party and its leader, President Saddam Hussein. Punishments for criticizing the regime include tongue amputations and the death penalty. The government exercises complete control over all domestic print and broadcast media, except in the Kurdish region in the north, where many independent newspapers have appeared over the past decade. Saddam Hussein's eldest son, Uday, manages about a dozen newspapers, including the most influential daily, *Babil*, which itself was the subject of a one-month suspension for having run editorials critical of the regime. Uday is also the director of all television and radio stations and is the head of the Journalists Union, to which all journalists are required to belong. Those foreign journalists allowed to work in Iraq are commonly accompanied by government officials who restrict their movements and their access to the public. Iraqis have limited access to foreign news programs such as those of the BBC, though the government regularly jammed broadcasters' signals. Internet access has become more available in recent years, but is frequently monitored and censored. [This report covers the time period of January to December 2002, and does not reflect changes to the situation in Iraq that have occurred in 2003.]

Ireland

Status: Free

LEGAL ENVIRONMENT: 5
POLITICAL INFLUENCES: 6
ECONOMIC PRESSURES: 5
TOTAL SCORE: 16

The state generally respects freedom of the press, and the constitution provides for freedom of expression unless the expression is deemed contrary to the public order or the authority of the state. Criminal libel laws and national security legislation result in isolated cases of self-censorship. Official censorship boards have the authority to ban books and movies for violent or pornographic content. Critics have charged that the country's censorship boards violate the European Convention of Human Rights. Print media are independent and offer a variety of perspectives. The government largely controls television broadcasts. However, the growth of cable and satellite providers has diminished the once-dominant influence of state television.

Israel

Status: Free

LEGAL ENVIRONMENT: 7
POLITICAL INFLUENCES: 12
ECONOMIC PRESSURES: 8
TOTAL SCORE: 27

Tensions between journalists and Israel's Government Press Office (GPO) increased significantly in 2002, as Palestinian terror attacks and Israeli reprisals intensified. The GPO, citing security concerns, did not renew the credentials of several Palestinian journalists. Press freedom organizations and Western news organizations—which rely heavily on Palestinian crews—demanded the accreditations be reinstated. The GPO declined to renew credentials after some Palestinian militants had posed as journalists in order to carry out attacks inside Israel. Israel also announced it would arrest Palestinians journalists working in Israel without proper documentation. An Arab cameraman working for the Reuters news agency was denied entry into Israel in the summer; the GPO said he lacked proper work documents and denied the move was discriminatory. Israeli trade unions voiced concern during the year that too many foreign cameramen were working in Israel. In December the Interior Ministry ordered the closure of the radical Islamic weekly *Sawt al-Haq wa Al-Hurriya*, published by the radical wing of the Islamic Movement in Israel. Newspaper and magazine articles on security matters are subject to a military censor, though the scope of permissible reporting is wide. Editors may appeal a censorship decision to a three-member tribunal that includes two civilians. Arabic-language publications are censored more frequently than are Hebrew-language ones. Newspapers are privately owned, and they freely criticize government policy. Broadcast media are run both privately and by the state and reflect a broad range of opinion. [The rating for Israel reflects the state of press freedom within Israel proper, not in the West Bank and Gaza Strip, which is covered in the following report on the Israeli-administered Territories/Palestinian Authority.]

Israeli-Administered Territories /Palestinian Authority

Status: Not Free

LEGAL ENVIRONMENT: 30
POLITICAL INFLUENCES: 38
ECONOMIC PRESSURES: 18
TOTAL SCORE: 86

Amidst the ongoing Palestinian *intifada* (uprising), international press freedom groups criticized Israel for barring journalists from certain areas of the West Bank, especially where troops of the Israel Defense Forces

(IDF) were engaged in combat. Journalists were caught in crossfire or shot at directly while reporting from conflict zones at various times during the year. In March, Italian freelance journalist Raffaele Ciriello was shot and killed by Israeli tank fire during a firefight with Palestinian militants in Ramallah; the Committee to Protect Journalists reported in September that more than 40 journalists had been hit by gunfire since the beginning of the uprising in September 2000. The IDF destroyed radio and television stations operated by the Palestinian Authority (PA). Official Palestinian media outlets often carry inflammatory broadcasts that encourage attacks against Israel. The IDF also arrested several Palestinian journalists on terrorism charges. Israel's Government Press Office, citing security concerns, did not renew the credentials of several Palestinian journalists in 2002. Western news organizations rely heavily on Palestinian crews, and press freedom organizations demanded the accreditations be reinstated. Press freedom groups also called upon the PA to cease harassment of journalists.

Journalists covering the intifada faced harassment during the year. Palestinian security officials reportedly threatened journalists who filed stories deemed unfavorable to the PA and Chairman Yasser Arafat. PA-affiliated militias warned Israeli journalists to stay out of Palestinian areas. In August, the Palestinian Journalists' Union and the Palestinian Journalists' Syndicate imposed a ban on the use of photographs depicting armed children and masked men. The ban was extended to foreign photographers. Under a 1995 Palestinian press law, journalists may be fined and jailed and newspapers closed for publishing "secret information" on Palestinian security forces, or news that might harm national unity or incite violence. However, another press law, also signed in 1995, stipulates that Palestinian intelligence services do not reserve the right to interrogate, detain, or arrest journalists on the basis of their work. Still, several small media outlets are pressured by authorities to provide favorable coverage of Arafat and the PA. Arbitrary arrests, threats, and the physical abuse of journalists critical of the PA are routine. Official Palestinian radio and television are government mouthpieces.

Italy

Status: Free

LEGAL ENVIRONMENT: 8
POLITICAL INFLUENCES: 6
ECONOMIC PRESSURES: 14
TOTAL SCORE: 28

The political use of libel suits and the further consolidation of national media interests threaten to undermine press freedom in Italy. In 2001, Italian courts ruled that both journalists and editors could be held responsible in defamation cases if they published potentially libelous statements gathered during an interview. Politicians frequently file libel suits against reporters and press organizations. During 2002, media outlets faced no less than $1.5 billion in potential damages from defamation suits. Also during the year, critics raised concerns about the continued erosion of media plurality in the country. Prime Minister Silvio Berlusconi's substantial family business holdings control Italy's three largest private television stations and one newspaper. In February 2002, his government appointed new members to the governing body of the state television broadcaster (RAI). In June, RAI canceled a popular television program that had frequently been critical of the prime minister. Several months later, RAI banned an unrelated television episode satirizing Berlusconi. By the end of the year, leading journalists at *Corriere della Sera*, Italy's largest daily, warned that a proposed corporate restructuring threatened to undermine the paper's editorial independence and further diminish media pluralism in the country.

Jamaica

Status: Free

LEGAL ENVIRONMENT: 3
POLITICAL INFLUENCES: 11
ECONOMIC PRESSURES: 6
TOTAL SCORE: 20

Jamaica enjoys freedom of the press, which is provided for in the constitution. Libel laws carrying prison terms remain on the books, although they are rarely enforced. The four largest newspapers, all privately owned, regularly report on alleged human rights abuses and frequently criticize the establishment. Journalists practice some self-censorship regarding corruption and rampant crime to avoid being threatened with harm, particularly by drug gangs and Colombian narcotics traffickers. There are three television stations and more than a dozen radio stations operating in the country. The Freedom of Information Act, passed in 2002, will allow public disclosure of official ministry documents but has been criticized for exempting cabinet-level documents from possible scrutiny.

Japan

Status: Free

LEGAL ENVIRONMENT: 2
POLITICAL INFLUENCES: 7
ECONOMIC PRESSURES: 8
TOTAL SCORE: 17

Press freedom is provided for in the constitution and generally upheld by an independent judiciary and functioning democratic political system. Japanese media and international press freedom groups expressed concern in 2002 about proposed legislation, including the Personal Data Protection Bill, that could potentially place restrictions on the press. Criticism of *kisha* clubs (exclusive, private, press clubs affiliated with public institutions, political parties, or large corporations) continued, with the EU calling the system a "restraint on the free trade in information." The clubs often provide major media outlets with exclusive access to news sources, while generally barring foreign and freelance reporters. Journalists sometimes practice self-censorship rather than report aggressively on sensitive financial issues.

Jordan

Status: Not Free

LEGAL ENVIRONMENT: 29
POLITICAL INFLUENCES: 21
ECONOMIC PRESSURES: 15
TOTAL SCORE: 65

Status change explanation: Jordan's rating changed from Partly Free to Not Free to reflect increasing restrictions imposed on the press in the aftermath of September 11, 2001.

The 1998 Press and Publications Law and its 1999 revisions constrain press freedom in the country. Journalists are frequently intimidated into practicing self-censorship and must be members of the Jordan Press Association to be considered legal practitioners. Restrictions on the press were tightened in the aftermath of the September 11, 2001, attacks on the United States, with the government broadening its authority to prosecute journalists and close publications. Under the guise of implementing antiterror efforts, authorities arrested several reporters throughout the year for having published "false information" or for criticizing the government or relations with neighboring states. The government also joined several other Arab countries in banning the Qatar-based satellite news channel Al-Jazeera from its territory, after the station aired a talk show in which speakers criticized Jordan's moderate policy on the Middle East. Three journalists were found guilty and received prison sentences for "libeling Islam's prophet and disparaging the dignity of the state." Two of the journalists were later released; however, one remains in jail. There are high taxes on the media industry and tariffs on paper, which some owners have claimed reduces the size of their publications. The government is the sole broadcaster of radio and television programs and must license all publications. The government has also been criticized for its policy of advertising primarily in newspapers in which it owns shares.

Kazakhstan

Status: Not Free

LEGAL ENVIRONMENT: 24
POLITICAL INFLUENCES: 27
ECONOMIC PRESSURES: 22
TOTAL SCORE: 73

President Nursultan Nazarbayev's crackdown on opposition media has prompted a further deterioration of press freedom. Existing legislation criminalizes insults against the "honor and dignity" of the president. Under the 1999 Law on Confidential State Affairs, the economic interests of Nazarbayev and his family officially became state secrets. While the regime had previously used such legislation to prosecute journalists for investigating corruption, state officials have recently begun to change tactics. Over the past year, prosecutors have charged opposition reporters with a variety of crimes involving narcotics, illegal weapons, and theft. In June 2002, the daughter of a leading opposition editor died while in police custody. The woman's mother had recently published an expose on several prominent government officials. Authorities claimed the death was a suicide. In October, law enforcement officials charged investigative journalist Sergei Duvanov with the rape of a 14-year-old girl. Human rights organizations have denounced the arrest as politically motivated. Self-censorship is widespread. Threats and physical assaults against journalists frequently remain unsolved. The Nazarbayev regime controls or otherwise influences most newspapers, printing and distribution facilities, and electronic broadcasts.

Legal Environment: 24
Political Influences: 24
Kenya
Economic Pressures: 20
Status: Not Free
Total Score: 68

The government routinely ignores constitutional guarantees of freedom of expression and broadly interprets several laws, including the Official Secrets Act, the penal code, and criminal libel laws, to restrict the press. In recent years, senior politicians have brought defamation charges against a number of media outlets and publishers, winning potentially crippling monetary awards, while journalists have been sentenced to prison terms. New legislation signed into law in June raised publishers' mandatory insurance bond to one million Kenyan shillings, required publishers to submit copies of their publications to a government registrar, and increased the penalties for noncompliance to include stiff fines as well as lengthy jail sentences for both publishers and vendors. Although official pressure and bribery led some journalists to practice self-censorship, the private print media are generally outspoken and critical of government policies. The state has somewhat loosened its grip over the broadcast media, but the government-controlled Kenya Broadcasting Corporation (KBC) remains dominant outside the major urban centers and its coverage favors the ruling party. Prior to the December 2002 national elections, KBC refused to broadcast the paid advertisements of the major opposition party. Reporters continue to face some harassment at the hands of police and other officials.

Legal Environment: 6
Political Influences: 4
Kiribati
Economic Pressures: 16
Status: Free
Total Score: 26

Freedom of the press is generally respected, although the government does limit this right in some instances. An amendment to the Newspaper Registration Act passed in October 2002 allows authorities to shut down newspapers if there are complaints made against them. Ieremia Tabai, a former president and current member of parliament, owns the sole independent newspaper, the *Kiribati New Star*. The state-owned Radio Kiribati offers foreign news broadcasts along with local programming. The opposition claimed that it had little access to Radio Kiribati and the government's *Te Uekera* weekly paper during the 2002 election campaign. In a positive development, Tabai said in December that he would begin operating a radio station in early 2003 after winning a four-year battle with the government to receive an FM license. The September 2000 ban on a foreign journalist remains in place.

Korea, North

LEGAL ENVIRONMENT: 30
POLITICAL INFLUENCES: 40
ECONOMIC PRESSURES: 26

Status: Not Free   TOTAL SCORE: 96

The government controls all media and information, and strictly curtails freedom of speech. Censorship is enforced, and the reporting on state-run media outlets does not deviate from the official line or cover sensitive topics. Ordinary North Koreans face a steady onslaught of propaganda from radios and televisions that are pre-tuned to receive only government stations. According to the Committee to Protect Journalists, the penal code cites listening to foreign broadcasts and possessing dissident publications as "crimes against the state," which are punishable by death. North Koreans have neither the right nor the means to access the Internet. Although more foreign journalists have been allowed into the country in the past two years, their movements within the country remain closely monitored and highly restricted.

Korea, South

LEGAL ENVIRONMENT: 7
POLITICAL INFLUENCES: 10
ECONOMIC PRESSURES: 12

Status: Free   TOTAL SCORE: 29

Freedom of expression is generally respected, although provisions in the National Security Law have been used to restrict the propagation of ideas that authorities consider Communist or pro–North Korean. Courts have in recent years jailed several journalists under criminal libel laws. Media rights groups say that politicians and businessmen use the libel laws to punish journalists for articles that are critical but factually accurate. In a controversial move, the National Tax Service in 2001 fined 23 media companies a record $390 million for tax evasion. Tax authorities also filed related criminal charges against five media executives and arrested three of them, including the owners of South Korea's two largest and more critical newspapers, *Chosun Ilbo* and *Dong-a Ilbo*. Both foreign and local observers differ over whether these media outlets were being targeted for their reporting or were simply being brought to book for tax evasion. Newspapers are privately owned and report fairly aggressively on governmental policies and alleged official wrongdoing. However, many are associated with substantial business interests, and journalists are also susceptible to bribery. Most broadcast media are state-subsidized, but offer diverse views.

Kuwait

Status: Partly Free

LEGAL ENVIRONMENT: 19
POLITICAL INFLUENCES: 22
ECONOMIC PRESSURES: 13
TOTAL SCORE: 54

The constitution provides for freedom of the press, and the media are free to scrutinize the government with some important exceptions. The Printing and Publications Law and the penal code restrict criticism of the emir and of relations with other states; material deemed offensive to religion; incitements to violence, hatred, or dissent; and news that affects the value of the national currency. These laws are arbitrarily enforced. Journalists commonly practice self-censorship in order to avoid being penalized under these laws. Broadcast media are government-owned, but access to foreign satellite stations is legal and widespread. A variety of privately owned newspapers exist. The government closed down the local offices of Arabic satellite television news channel Al-Jazeera after the station reported on U.S.-Kuwaiti military exercises. The government claimed that the report harmed the country's interests and that the station lacked professionalism and objectivity when dealing with Kuwaiti issues.

Kyrgyzstan

Status: Not Free

LEGAL ENVIRONMENT: 23
POLITICAL INFLUENCES: 26
ECONOMIC PRESSURES: 22
TOTAL SCORE: 71

Freedom of the press declined in 2002 as a result of the government's attempts to introduce new restrictions on independent media. Although

Articles 15 and 16 of the constitution provide for freedom of expression and the press, local journalists do not fully enjoy these rights. In recent years, the administration of President Askar Akayev, increasingly impatient with critics of the regime, has taken a number of steps to curb or control opposition media outlets. Libel is a criminal offense and journalists face the threat of harsh fines and prison terms. The Law on Mass Media contains similar restrictions on defamation. Consequently, self-censorship is common among media professionals. A 2001 decree made it easier for the state to imprison critical reporters. In January 2002, a separate decree prohibited the operation of independent printing presses for the first five months of the year. During this time, the state publishing house refused to print the independent newspapers *Res Publika* and *Moya Stolitsa*. Nearly 70 percent of all media outlets are in private hands. Yet unlike state-sponsored media, few private outlets reach a national audience. Internet publications are becoming increasingly popular and serve to partially bypass the temporary restrictions on independent printing. Nevertheless, Internet use is generally limited to the capital.

Laos

LEGAL ENVIRONMENT: 26
POLITICAL INFLUENCES: 31
ECONOMIC PRESSURES: 23

Status: Not Free

TOTAL SCORE: 80

Press freedom is provided for by the constitution but is severely restricted in practice. Provisions in the penal code broadly forbid inciting disorder, slandering the state, distorting state policies, or disseminating information or opinions that weaken the state. In addition, the law subjects journalists who do not file "constructive reports" or who attempt to "obstruct" the ruling party's work to jail terms of up to 15 years. Foreign journalists must apply for special visas and are restricted in their activities, and foreign news reports appearing in Lao publications are subject to censorship. The government owns all newspapers and broadcast media, and tightly controls their content. Authorities also control all domestic Internet servers, and sporadically monitor e-mail and block access to some political Web sites. In October, authorities opened the first government-run Internet center in Vientiane.

LEGAL ENVIRONMENT: 7
POLITICAL INFLUENCES: 5

Latvia

ECONOMIC PRESSURES: 6

Status: Free

TOTAL SCORE: 18

Article 100 of the constitution bans censorship and guarantees freedom of expression. Local journalists enjoy these rights in practice. During 2002, there were no reported violations of press freedom. Latvian media exist without substantial government regulation; however, broadcasters are required to limit non-Latvian-language programming to 25 percent of their total airtime. In the last decade, strong economic competition has primarily fueled the development of domestic mass media. With the exception of two state-run weeklies, all Latvian newspapers are privately owned. The majority of television and radio broadcasters are also in private hands. The state-run Latvijas Radio maintains the largest national radio audience, while the private TV Latvijas Neatkariga Televizija holds the largest national viewing audience. Internet access is open and unrestricted.

LEGAL ENVIRONMENT: 25
POLITICAL INFLUENCES: 29

Lebanon

ECONOMIC PRESSURES: 17

Status: Not Free

TOTAL SCORE: 71

Although journalists are allowed to generally scrutinize government officials and policies, strict security and defamation laws severely constrain press freedom, and the law prohibits attacks on the dignity of the head of state or foreign leaders. The government may prosecute offending journalists in the Publications Court, a special tribunal that oversees press issues. Authorities frequently exert pressure on journalists to practice self-censorship through harassment and intimidation. Most television and radio stations are privately owned, but the government decides who can operate these stations and whether or not they can broadcast news. Nevertheless, broadcasting is more diverse than in other Arab countries. Widespread protest followed the closing of an independent television station and its affiliate radio station after a court accused the stations of violating a law against broadcasting political propaganda during elections. Critics of the closure say it was aimed at silencing criticism of the pro-Syrian government and Syria. Media outlets often reflect the opinions of their financial backers.

LEGAL ENVIRONMENT: 11
POLITICAL INFLUENCES: 15

Lesotho
ECONOMIC PRESSURES: 16

Status: Partly Free
TOTAL SCORE: 42

The government generally respects freedom of speech and the press, which is provided for in the constitution. However, a 1938 proclamation prohibits criticism of the government and contains liabilities for seditious libel. Journalists and media organizations are regularly the targets of defamation lawsuits; in December, a private company sued a weekly tabloid for publishing damaging information. A number of independent newspapers, including Christian publications and four English-language weeklies, freely scrutinize government policies. However, state-owned print and broadcast media reflect the views of the ruling party and do not give equal coverage to opposition parties. Journalists reportedly have trouble gaining free access to official information. Media development remains constrained by underfunding and a lack of resources.

LEGAL ENVIRONMENT: 22
POLITICAL INFLUENCES: 34

Liberia
ECONOMIC PRESSURES: 23

Status: Not Free
TOTAL SCORE: 79

President Charles Taylor's regime continues to sharply restrict the operation of the press, disregarding the constitutional right to freedom of expression. In February, the government introduced a state of emergency that broadened its powers to clamp down on dissent, announcing that those who criticized the decree would be "dealt with" under the new emergency laws. Authorities shut down *The Analyst*, a leading independent daily, several times during 2002 under the new legislation. Individual journalists continued to be the targets of official harassment, persistent surveillance, and arbitrary arrest and detention. The most prominent, Hassan Bility, editor of *The Analyst*, was arrested in June, labeled an "unlawful combatant," and held incommunicado without charge or trial. Following diplomatic intervention from the United States, he was released in December into the custody of the U.S. embassy in Monrovia. The president owns or controls nearly all print and broadcast media, as well as Liberia's only printing press. Critical news outlets have been threatened by a withdrawal of advertising or have been prosecuted for tax evasion. In this restrictive environment, many journalists practice self-censorship.

Libya

Status: Not Free

LEGAL ENVIRONMENT: 28
POLITICAL INFLUENCES: 34
ECONOMIC PRESSURES: 27
TOTAL SCORE: 89

Colonel Mu'ammar al-Qadhafi continues his campaign for international respectability, and members of the international press continue to report fewer restrictions on their movement and less government interference. Still, the state of press freedom in Libya is dismal. The government restricts the ability of the media to operate freely by prohibiting all political activities not officially approved; by enacting vaguely worded laws that may interpret many forms of speech or expression as illegal; and by operating a system of informants that creates mistrust at all levels of society. The whereabouts of journalist Abdullah Ali al-Sanussi al-Darat, who has been detained without trial or charges brought against him since 1973 is still unknown. In April the press announced that the Government had revoked writer Farag Sayyid Bul-Isha's citizenship as a punishment for his participation in a program on Al-Jazeera. The state owns and controls the country's media outlets, and the authorities do not permit the publication of opinions contrary to government policy. Foreign programming is available through satellite, although some programs are censored.

Liechtenstein

Status: Free

LEGAL ENVIRONMENT: 2
POLITICAL INFLUENCES: 3
ECONOMIC PRESSURES: 6
TOTAL SCORE: 11

Article 40 of the constitution guarantees freedom of expression and the press. During 2002, there were no reported violations of press freedom. Existing legislation attempts to maintain a diversity of viewpoints in the media, and an independent state commission provides subsidies to the press. The principality's two daily newspapers, *Liechtensteiner Vaterland* and *Liechtensteiner Volksblatt*, generally reflect the views of the two main political parties. A private television company competes with the state broadcaster. The sole radio station is privately owned. Broadcasts from neighboring Switzerland and Austria are widely available. Internet access is open and unrestricted.

Lithuania
Status: Free

LEGAL ENVIRONMENT: 7
POLITICAL INFLUENCES: 5
ECONOMIC PRESSURES: 6
TOTAL SCORE: 18

Article 25 of the constitution bans censorship and guarantees freedom of expression. Local journalists generally enjoy these rights in practice. Libel remains a criminal offense, although there were no reported cases during the year. In October, the Constitutional Court ruled that judicial authorities may compel journalists to reveal confidential sources. While media outlets are free from direct state interference, the government has recently curtailed access to public information, such as draft legislation, and limited press access to cabinet officials. All newspapers and magazines are privately owned. Private corporations control three of the four national TV networks and all but three radio stations. The public broadcaster, Lithuanian Radio and Television (LRTV), operates on a mixture of direct state funding, licensing fees, and advertising revenue. At present, there is a drive to replace LRTV's advertising revenue with a subscriber's fee. Internet access is open and unrestricted.

Luxembourg
Status: Free

LEGAL ENVIRONMENT: 3
POLITICAL INFLUENCES: 3
ECONOMIC PRESSURES: 8
TOTAL SCORE: 14

During 2002, the media enjoyed constitutional protections for a free press. Newspapers and magazines present a diverse spectrum of viewpoints, yet many are aligned with major political parties or trade unions. The country's small size limits advertising revenue. Since 1976, the government has heavily subsidized media outlets to prevent closures. The country's size has likewise prevented the growth of new radio and television broadcasters. A single media conglomerate dominates the broadcast market.

Macedonia

Status: Partly Free

LEGAL ENVIRONMENT: 12
POLITICAL INFLUENCES: 19
ECONOMIC PRESSURES: 19
TOTAL SCORE: 50

Freedom of the press declined for a second consecutive year, as a result of increased state pressure on independent media. Article 16 of the constitution bans censorship and guarentees freedom of expression. However, Macedonian media do not always enjoy these rights in practice. Libel remains a criminal offense. In early September 2002, the Interior Ministry threatened media professionals with criminal prosecution if they "disgraced" the ruling party in the run-up to parliamentary elections. Days later, authorities filed criminal libel charges against magazine journalist Marjan Djurovski. The parliamentary campaign exposed several problems related to state influence. News coverage at state-run Macedonian Radio and Television was biased in favor of the government, a violation of existing legislation. Some private broadcasters likewise exhibited slanted political coverage; others were forcibly closed for the duration of the campaign. The government-controlled publisher Nova Makedonija drastically reduced the price of the pro-government newspaper *Vecer*, thereby creating an unfair advantage over the financially troubled opposition press. In one case of violence, armed activists attacked an opposition publishing house. Journalists sometimes experience harassment, arbitrary detention, and abuse at the hands of police.

Madagascar

Status: Partly Free

LEGAL ENVIRONMENT: 7
POLITICAL INFLUENCES: 19
ECONOMIC PRESSURES: 12
TOTAL SCORE: 38

Political turmoil following the hotly contested December 2001 presidential election took its toll on the media during the first half of 2002. In February, President Didier Ratsiraka declared a state of emergency, which empowered authorities to take control of news broadcasting. Threats and violent attacks directed at members of the press and media outlets increased sharply during the crisis, but largely subsided by July. A number of daily and weekly newspapers publish material critical of the government and other parties and politicians. However, authorities occasionally pressure media outlets to curb their coverage of certain issues, opposition politicians are rarely given access to state-run media, and some journalists practice self-censorship. Although nationwide radio and television broadcasting remains a state monopoly, a large number of local, privately owned stations operate across the country.

Malawi
Status: Partly Free

LEGAL ENVIRONMENT: 17
POLITICAL INFLUENCES: 24
ECONOMIC PRESSURES: 16
TOTAL SCORE: 57

Freedom of speech and of the press is legally guaranteed and generally respected in practice. However, the independent media did face growing restrictions and harassment at the hands of the government and its supporters during the year. Defamation charges as well as charges based on other laws have been used to prosecute members of the press. As a result, some journalists practice self-censorship. Although a broad spectrum of opinion is presented in some two dozen private newspapers, the state-owned Malawi Broadcasting Corporation controls television and most radio service, where coverage favors the ruling party. Reporters and media outlets faced verbal threats as well as physical attacks at the hands of police, senior politicians, and supporters of the ruling party throughout 2002, most commonly because of their opposition to President Elson Muluzi's attempt to run for a third term in office. Other forms of official intimidation included a threat to withdraw the broadcasting license of a community radio station and the impounding of a publishing house's assets.

Malaysia
Status: Not Free

LEGAL ENVIRONMENT: 26
POLITICAL INFLUENCES: 27
ECONOMIC PRESSURES: 18
TOTAL SCORE: 71

Limitations on freedom of expression are permitted by the constitution, and the media remained sharply constrained by legal restrictions and official intimidation in 2002. The Printing Presses and Publications Act requires all publishers and printing firms to obtain an annual permit to operate, which can be withdrawn without judicial review. Some pro-opposition media outlets have been shut down. The Official Secrets Act, the Sedition Act, and the Broadcasting Act also impose wide restrictions on freedom of expression.

Businessmen and companies close to the ruling coalition own most major newspapers, and political news coverage and editorials strongly support the government line. Government pressure was suspected when more than 40 journalists were laid off or resigned from *The Sun* newspaper after it published a politically sensitive story in December 2001. Authorities have also increased official pressure on Malaysiakini.com, an online news daily. Foreign publications are subject to censorship, and issues containing critical articles are frequently delayed. State-run Radio Television Malaysia and the two private television stations offer flattering coverage of the government and rarely air opposition views. Many journalists practice self-censorship. Journalist Hishamuddin Rais, who was detained under the Internal Security Act in 2001, remains incarcerated.

Maldives
Status: Not Free

LEGAL ENVIRONMENT: 24
POLITICAL INFLUENCES: 22
ECONOMIC PRESSURES: 18
TOTAL SCORE: 64

Press freedom is restricted by a strict legal code that the government did not hesitate to enforce in 2002. The law authorizes officials to close newspapers and sanction journalists for insulting Islam, threatening national security, or publishing libelous statements. The penal code bans speech and publications that could "arouse people against the government," while other regulations make editors criminally responsible for the content of the material they publish. Four Internet writers were arrested early in the year, and after being held in detention and charged with defamation in May, three were sentenced to life imprisonment. In this environment, many journalists practice self-censorship, although some private newspapers criticize government policy. All broadcast media are owned and operated by the government.

Mali
Status: Free

LEGAL ENVIRONMENT: 6
POLITICAL INFLUENCES: 9
ECONOMIC PRESSURES: 9
TOTAL SCORE: 24

Freedom of speech and of the press is guaranteed in the constitution and is generally respected. However, several laws provide for substantial penalties, including imprisonment, for libel and public injury. At least 40 private newspapers operate freely, and more than 100 independent radio stations, including community stations broadcasting in regional languages, broadcast throughout the country. The state controls the only television station and a number of radio stations, but all present diverse views, including those critical of the government. Journalists, particularly those who report on corruption issues, remain subject to some intimidation and pressure at the hands of authorities and unidentified assailants.

Malta

Status: Free

LEGAL ENVIRONMENT: 2
POLITICAL INFLUENCES: 4
ECONOMIC PRESSURES: 7
TOTAL SCORE: 13

Section 41 of the constitution guarantees freedom of expression, and the media enjoy these rights in practice. The Press Act of 1996 further expanded press freedom, allowing for free access to official information and protection of confidential sources. The Broadcasting Act 1991 opened the way for a wide variety of radio and television stations. The government has further amended this law in accordance with EU requirements. In contrast to the diversity in the broadcast sector, print media are generally limited to political and religious newspapers. Internet access is open and unrestricted, yet Malta has one of the lowest usage rates in Europe.

Marshall Islands

Status: Free

LEGAL ENVIRONMENT: 0
POLITICAL INFLUENCES: 5
ECONOMIC PRESSURES: 5
TOTAL SCORE: 10

The constitution provides for freedom of the press, and the government generally respects this right in practice. The *Marshall Islands Gazette*, a government monthly, carries official announcements and tends to avoid political coverage. In addition, journalists practice some self-censorship on sensitive political issues. The media consist of a private weekly newspaper, which prints articles in both English and Marshallese, and two radio stations: the state broadcaster and a station that offers religious broadcasting along with news from the BBC and other foreign services. In addition, a cable station carries entertainment, foreign news, and coverage of local events.

Mauritania

LEGAL ENVIRONMENT: 21
POLITICAL INFLUENCES: 23
ECONOMIC PRESSURES: 17

Status: Not Free   TOTAL SCORE: 61

The constitution provides for freedom of expression, but the 1991 press law forbids the publication or dissemination of reports deemed to "attack the principles of Islam or the credibility of the state, harm the general interest, or disturb public order and security." All publishers must register with the Interior Ministry and submit copies of newspapers to the ministry for review and possible prepublication censorship. A number of newspapers were banned or seized during the year. Journalists are also sometimes subjected to harassment and arbitrary arrest at the hands of authorities. Independent print media outlets openly criticize the government. However, state-owned media outlets, including two daily newspapers as well as radio and television broadcasters, slant coverage to favor the ruling party and sometimes limit opposition parties' access. Foreign television broadcasts are available via satellite, and a number of Internet service providers operate without government restrictions.

Mauritius

LEGAL ENVIRONMENT: 5
POLITICAL INFLUENCES: 9
ECONOMIC PRESSURES: 10

Status: Free   TOTAL SCORE: 24

Press freedom is guaranteed in the constitution and is generally observed. Strict libel laws have not been used to inhibit the media. The Independent Broadcast Authority, established in 2001 and chaired by a government appointee, is mandated to regulate and license all radio and television broadcasting. A small number of private radio stations have been authorized to operate, but the state-run media enjoy a monopoly in broadcasting local news and generally reflect official views. A number of private daily and weekly publications, however, are often highly critical of both government and opposition politicians and their policies.

Mexico
Status: Partly Free

LEGAL ENVIRONMENT: 13
POLITICAL INFLUENCES: 16
ECONOMIC PRESSURES: 9
TOTAL SCORE: 38

The situation of press freedom further improved in 2002 as the administration of President Vincente Fox continued to enact democratic reforms. The country's first freedom-of-information law was passed; it will allow citizens access to nearly all federal government information with the exception of information on private citizens or that which is considered vital to national security. Libel, however, remains a criminal offense, and there were several cases during the year of journalists being prosecuted under defamation laws. Several journalists were threatened or harassed for having reported on official corruption or the criminal activities of drug cartels, and at least two journalists were murdered because of their work. In an attempt to review the status of inquiries into crimes against journalists, the Government Ministry has set up a review board that includes representatives of human rights and press organizations to work through the cases. Media outlets, which are mostly private, are largely dependent on the government for advertising revenues. There were reports in the states of Chiapas and Baja California that the government had withdrawn advertising funds in response to unfavorable coverage. Television news independence has been enhanced by greater political pluralism, and the media have shown a high degree of editorial independence. Bribery of journalists, which was common in the past, is on the decline.

Micronesia
Status: Free

LEGAL ENVIRONMENT: 2
POLITICAL INFLUENCES: 3
ECONOMIC PRESSURES: 12
TOTAL SCORE: 17

Press freedom is constitutionally guaranteed and generally respected. The *Island Tribune*, an independent weekly, covers politically diverse issues, but other newspapers tend to avoid controversial topics. The media consist of government newsletters, several small private papers, television stations in three of the four states, radio stations run by each of the four state governments, and a radio station run by a religious group. Satellite television is increasingly available, and there is an increasing level of discussion of sensitive issues on various Internet sites.

Moldova

Status: Partly Free

LEGAL ENVIRONMENT: 20
POLITICAL INFLUENCES: 22
ECONOMIC PRESSURES: 17
TOTAL SCORE: 59

Independent media in Moldova face obstacles from restrictive libel laws, government pressure, and dependence upon state financing. Article 32 of the constitution guarantees freedom of expression and the press. However, existing legislation prohibits insults against the state and defamation of senior government officials. These provisions have allowed for a multitude of lawsuits against journalists in the dozen years since independence. Consequently, self-censorship is common among journalists. Media professionals regularly risk harassment or physical assault, especially when reporting on corruption. In October, police arrested the chief editor and two reporters at the independent newspaper *Accente*. The paper was preparing to publish an investigative report on the director of the state security service. Earlier in the year, nearly 400 reporters at TeleRadio Moldova, the state television and radio broadcaster, held demonstrations to protest alleged censorship and demand greater independence for the media. The government eventually transferred control of TeleRadio Moldova to an independent corporation. Yet, questions remain over the editorial independence of this new body, as it will derive its sole funding from the state budget. The majority of print and broadcast outlets are privately owned but are nevertheless not entirely independent of government influence.

Monaco

Status: Free

LEGAL ENVIRONMENT: 3
POLITICAL INFLUENCES: 2
ECONOMIC PRESSURES: 4
TOTAL SCORE: 9

Article 23 of the constitution guarantees freedom of expression, and the local press enjoys these rights in practice. The penal code prohibits insults against the monarch and royal family. Aside from limited examples of self-censorship related to these restrictions, there were no reported press freedom violations during 2002. Monaco has no domestic daily newspapers; however, French papers, which are widely available, cover developments in the principality. The government produces a weekly news bulletin. There is one private television station. Foreign radio and television broadcasts are easily received. Internet access is open and unrestricted.

Mongolia

Status: Partly Free

LEGAL ENVIRONMENT: 11
POLITICAL INFLUENCES: 11
ECONOMIC PRESSURES: 14
TOTAL SCORE: 36

The government generally respects press freedom, which is provided for in the constitution. A 1998 media law bans the censorship of public information and also requires authorities to privatize all media. However, this latter provision had not yet been implemented by year's end, and some broadcast media remain under state control. Libel is a criminal offense, and the law places the burden of proof on defendants in defamation cases. In August, an editor was sentenced to one year's imprisonment for publishing false information. Mongolian media offer a range of independent and party views that often are critical of the government, but some outlets practice self-censorship. The press claims that their is indirect censorship through frequent government libel lawsuits and tax audits following critical articles. In addition, lack of access to information continues to hamper investigative journalism.

Morocco

LEGAL ENVIRONMENT: 19
POLITICAL INFLUENCES: 22
ECONOMIC PRESSURES: 16

Status: Partly Free

TOTAL SCORE: 57

The government does not tolerate criticism of the monarchy, of Morocco's claim to the Western Sahara, or of Islam. The 1973 press code gives the authorities the power to censor newspapers and directly order them not to report on certain issues. A new media law promulgated in 2002 reduces jail terms stipulated by the press code, makes it easier to launch a publication, and requires the government to give reasons for confiscations, but the Moroccan Press Union condemned the measure for not eliminating penal sanctions entirely. Despite this new law, several foreign publications were confiscated, along with some domestic publications. In addition, the law still provides for jail sentences and fines for journalists found guilty of libeling public officials. In February, the editor and director of the *Journal Hebdomadaire* were convicted for defamation and sentenced to jail terms and steep fines. The number and severity of punitive actions against journalists and publications declined somewhat in 2002, though there were several instances of journalists being detained, questioned, and intimidated as a result of their reporting. Broadcast media, which are mostly government-controlled, reflect official views, though foreign broadcasting is available via satellite and a large independent print press flourishes.

Mozambique

LEGAL ENVIRONMENT: 14
POLITICAL INFLUENCES: 18
ECONOMIC PRESSURES: 15

Status: Partly Free

TOTAL SCORE: 47

The 1990 constitution provides for press freedom, but limits this right in relation to respect for the constitution, human dignity, the imperatives of foreign policy, and national defense. Some journalists have alleged that the Higher Council of Social Communication, an enforcement body for the press law dominated by the ruling party, has attempted to promote self-censorship among members of the press. Criminal libel laws are sometimes used to prosecute media outlets for defamation, which serves as another important deterrent to open expression. The private media have enjoyed moderate growth, but publications in Maputo have little influence on the largely illiterate rural population. The state owns or influences all of the largest newspapers and also controls nearly all broadcast media. Although state-owned media have displayed greater editorial independence in recent years, the opposition receives inadequate coverage on national radio and television. Reporters continue to be subjected to some threats and intimidation at the hands of officials. In November, the trial of six men accused of the November 2000 murder of investigative journalist Carlos Cardoso opened under tight security and domestic and international scrutiny.

Namibia

Status: Partly Free

LEGAL ENVIRONMENT: 8
POLITICAL INFLUENCES: 15
ECONOMIC PRESSURES: 14
TOTAL SCORE: 37

The constitution guarantees the right to free speech and a free press, but these rights are not always respected. In recent years, defamation lawsuits and other forms of legal action have been filed against several newspapers. Independent newspapers and radio stations continue to criticize the government openly. However, journalists at state-run media outlets have reportedly been subjected to indirect and direct pressure to avoid reporting on controversial topics, and they consequently practice self-censorship. Last year's official advertising and purchasing bans on *The Namibian*, a leading daily newspaper, remained in place. In August, President Sam Nujoma appointed himself minister of information and broadcasting, prompting fears that he intended to assert further official control over the state-owned Namibian Broadcasting Corporation, which operates most television and radio services.

Nauru

Status: Free

LEGAL ENVIRONMENT: 5
POLITICAL INFLUENCES: 11
ECONOMIC PRESSURES: 10
TOTAL SCORE: 26

Freedom of the press is generally respected, although the government occasionally limits this right. The August 2001 ban preventing a foreign reporter from entering the country remains in place. Nauru has no regular print media, but several publications appear on an occasional basis. They include a government bulletin and a newsletter called *The Visionary* that is often critical of the government. The sole radio station is government-owned and broadcasts Radio Australia and BBC news reports. The state-run Nauru TV and a privately owned sports network provide television service.

Nepal

Status: Not Free

Legal Environment: 19
Political Influences: 34
Economic Pressures: 12

Total Score: 65

Status change explanation: Nepal's rating moved from Partly Free to Not Free to reflect the worsening pressures placed on the media by both the government and Maoist rebels.

Conditions for journalists deteriorated sharply in 2002 as the Maoist insurgency escalated. Both the constitution and the Press and Publications Act broadly suppress speech and writing that could undermine the monarchy, national security, public order, or interethnic or intercaste relations. Emergency regulations imposed in November 2001 restricted press and publication rights as well as access to information, and journalists were requested by the government not to write articles "sympathetic" to the Maoist rebels. Since the state of emergency was declared, authorities have arrested over 150 journalists, and more than two dozen remained in detention at year's end, according to the Center for Human Rights and Democratic Studies. Several have reportedly been subjected to harassment and torture. In June, the editor of a pro-Maoist weekly died in police custody, while Maoists abducted and murdered two reporters during the year and threatened many others. However, in November, 14 journalists filed cases against the government seeking compensation for their illegal detentions. While many private publications continue to criticize government policies and corruption, self-censorship as a result of official intimidation is a growing concern. The government owns the influential Radio Nepal, whose political coverage favors the ruling party, as well as the sole television station.

LEGAL ENVIRONMENT: 5
POLITICAL INFLUENCES: 4

Netherlands
ECONOMIC PRESSURES: 6

Status: Free
TOTAL SCORE: 15

The constitution provides for freedom of expression and the press. Although the relevant laws are rarely enforced, journalists face imprisonment for insults against the monarch and royal family. Newspaper ownership is concentrated; nevertheless, the print media maintain a plurality of viewpoints. A 1988 broadcast law eliminated the ban on commercial broadcasting. Dutch viewers have access to a wide range of domestic and foreign channels. In a remnant of the traditional "pillar system," the state allocates public radio and television programming to political, religious, and social groups according to their membership size. Internet access is open and unrestricted.

LEGAL ENVIRONMENT: 1
POLITICAL INFLUENCES: 1

New Zealand
ECONOMIC PRESSURES: 6

Status: Free
TOTAL SCORE: 8

Press freedom is provided for by law and is respected, although access to information is not guaranteed. In December 2001, the government backed down from a plan to include a criminal defamation clause in the Electoral Amendment Bill. Independent broadcasters compete with state-owned radio and television, and New Zealand's private newspapers and magazines cover politics tenaciously, offering a range of views. Media organizations criticized the April 2002 decision of the high court to ban the *National Business Review* from reporting on a high-profile case involving a biotech firm.

LEGAL ENVIRONMENT: 10
POLITICAL INFLUENCES: 16

Nicaragua
ECONOMIC PRESSURES: 14

Status: Partly Free
TOTAL SCORE: 40

Privately owned print and broadcast media present diverse viewpoints and openly scrutinize the government. The constitution provides for press freedom, but several provisions serve as constraints on this right. While citizens have the right to "accurate" information, the government has the right to deem what is accurate. There is also the potential for criminal sanctions against journalists who commit libel, and laws require journalists to reveal their sources under special circumstances, though these laws are rarely enforced. President Enrique Bolanos has proven to be less confrontational with the press than his predecessor, Arnoldo Aleman. The new government is said to be treating newspapers more fairly— distributing advertising dollars according to circulation rather than following the previous practice of showing bias towards pro-government papers. However, despite its more favorable relationship with the press, the new government did shut down an opposition radio station that featured a program by the former president making attacks on the new administration.

Niger

Status: Partly Free

LEGAL ENVIRONMENT: 21
POLITICAL INFLUENCES: 17
ECONOMIC PRESSURES: 15
TOTAL SCORE: 53

Rights to freedom of expression and of the press are not always supported in practice, though the constitution guarantees such rights. Libel and slander are regarded as criminal acts, and are punished by imprisonment as well as fines. A number of journalists were arrested and detained throughout the year for allegedly insulting government officials. In June, the publication director of the satirical weekly *Le Canard Dechainé* was sentenced to eight months in prison on libel charges. In addition, the government cracked down on the press following an armed forces mutiny in August. A presidential decree had banned "the propagation of information or allegations likely to be detrimental to the implementation of national defense operations" and had threatened media outlets with suspension or closure if they violated the ban. Authorities detained two reporters for their coverage of the mutiny and held both without charge. Although coverage in the state-owned broadcast and print media reflects official priorities, a number of private publications freely criticize the government. The Committee to Protect Journalists reported that in late 2001, the press corps expressed concern over a new finance law that imposed heavy taxes on private news outlets.

Nigeria

Status: Partly Free

LEGAL ENVIRONMENT: 15
POLITICAL INFLUENCES: 22
ECONOMIC PRESSURES: 16
TOTAL SCORE: 53

Freedom of speech and expression is guaranteed, and the government generally respects these rights in practice. However, a number of legal restrictions continue to hinder the freedom of the press. Passed in 1999, Decree 60 created the government-appointed Nigerian Press Council and gave it the power to accredit journalists and register newspapers. In addition, criminal defamation laws are still used against journalists. In the largely Muslim northern states, Islamic law imposes additional penalties for alleged press offenses. Nevertheless, numerous independent publications provide a wide spectrum of views, and several private radio and television stations broadcast with little government interference. In February, officials granted broadcast licenses to 5 new television companies and 16 private radio stations. Reporters remain subject to occasional instances of intimidation, harassment, and arbitrary arrest at the hands of state governments, the police, and other actors. An article published in the private daily *ThisDay* sparked religious riots in November in which several hundred people were killed, while the newspaper's Kaduna office was burned down and Islamic authorities in the state of Zamfara called for the author of the article to be put to death. Journalists are often not paid in a timely manner, and some are susceptible to bribery. After *Time* magazine reported in April that some officials tried to bribe foreign reporters with cash, the government threatened to prosecute any foreign correspondent who wrote "malicious falsehoods" about the country.

Norway

Status: Free

LEGAL ENVIRONMENT: 2
POLITICAL INFLUENCES: 1
ECONOMIC PRESSURES: 6
TOTAL SCORE: 9

The constitution provides robust protections for freedom of the press. By law, insults against the flag or country may draw a prison term, as may defamation of the king or regent. Such laws are rarely enforced, however. In a nation of nearly 4.5 million people, Norway maintains more than

200 newspapers. At the same time, three large companies dominate the country's print media. The state provides direct subsidies to newspapers. These payments account for just 3 to 4 percent of most newspapers' total revenue and serve to limit the impact of local monopolies. Despite varied attempts, the government has not yet been able to reverse the trend of ownership concentration.

Oman

Status: Not Free

LEGAL ENVIRONMENT: 26
POLITICAL INFLUENCES: 25
ECONOMIC PRESSURES: 22
TOTAL SCORE: 73

There are no laws providing for press freedom in Oman. The 1996 basic charter, which would provide for broader press freedoms, has yet to be implemented. It is illegal to criticize the sultan in any form, but some scrutiny of government officials and agencies is tolerated. The government controls the only local radio and two television stations. There are several independent publications, but the government subsidizes their operating costs which discourages reporting on most major domestic issues. State broadcasts do not air any politically sensitive material, and the government has the right to censor print media and foreign publications. Such action is usually not necessary since self-censorship is widely practiced. Citizens have access to satellite television, including the popular Arabic news channel Al-Jazeera. Internet services are available through the nationally owned tele-communications company, though pornographic and politically sensitive sites are blocked.

Pakistan

Status: Partly Free

LEGAL ENVIRONMENT: 17
POLITICAL INFLUENCES: 25
ECONOMIC PRESSURES: 16
TOTAL SCORE: 58

The constitution and other laws authorize the government to curb freedom of speech on subjects including the constitution, the armed forces, the judiciary, and religion. Concern was raised that three ordinances adopted in August—the Press Council Ordinance, the Registration Ordinance, and the Defamation Ordinance—will further restrict freedom of expression. During the year,

Islamic fundamentalists and thugs hired by feudal landlords continued to harass journalists and attack newspaper offices. On several occasions, journalists were also subjected to physical attacks by police and political activists. The kidnap and murder of *Wall Street Journal* reporter Daniel Pearl by Islamic militants in early 2002 focused international attention on the dangers of reporting in Pakistan. While journalists practice some self-censorship, the independent press continues to present outspoken and diverse viewpoints. However, President Pervez Musharraf appeared to have become less tolerant of criticism. In March, editor Shaheen Sehbai resigned under pressure and left the country after *The News* published a story on the links between Pearl's killers and official intelligence agencies. He and his family continued to face legal harassment throughout the year. Other prominent editors also complained of receiving threats from intelligence agencies. Nearly all broadcast media are state-owned, and coverage favors the government.

Palau

LEGAL ENVIRONMENT: 0
POLITICAL INFLUENCES: 2
ECONOMIC PRESSURES: 7

Status: Free

TOTAL SCORE: 9

The constitution provides for freedom of the press, and the government generally respects this right in practice. The media consist of a government gazette, several independent weekly newspapers, one government-owned and three private radio stations, and cable television. While media outlets express a range of opinions, government media must also carry official views as part of their coverage.

Panama

LEGAL ENVIRONMENT: 16
POLITICAL INFLUENCES: 11
ECONOMIC PRESSURES: 7

Status: Partly Free

TOTAL SCORE: 34

Status change explanation: Panama's rating slipped from Free to Partly Free as a result of continued legal pressures on journalists and media outlets.

Panama has one of the highest levels of legal prosecution against the press in the Americas. Restrictive laws that were enacted during the regime of dictator General Manuel Antonio Noriega have yet to be repealed by three subsequent democratic governments. The law permits officials to jail without trial anyone who defames the government. In addition, legislation that will require journalists to be licensed is currently under consideration. The practice of self-censorship is on the rise as a result of the prosecution of journalists under restrictive gag laws. Nevertheless, media are abundant and diverse; a half dozen national daily newspapers and television stations and more than 100 radio stations offer an array of coverage and opinions. All media outlets are privately owned with the exception of one state-owned television station. However, there is a noticeable concentration of control of television outlets by associates and close relatives of former president Ernesto Perez Balladares.

Papua New Guinea
Status: Free

LEGAL ENVIRONMENT: 3
POLITICAL INFLUENCES: 10
ECONOMIC PRESSURES: 12
TOTAL SCORE: 25

Media freedom is provided for by law and is generally observed. The private press reports vigorously on alleged official corruption, police abuse, and other sensitive matters. However, journalists face occasional harassment and threats at the hands of the police and armed forces. Radio is a key source of information, given the country's low literacy rate and many isolated villages. State-run radio networks suffer from inadequate funding and deteriorating equipment, but offer balanced news coverage. The private NAU-FM network serves the capital of Port Moresby and is expanding into other areas, while local stations serve other cities. Television reception is limited mainly to Port Moresby and provincial capitals. In March, Reporters Sans Frontieres reported that foreign journalists were hindered in their attempts to visit refugee camps set up by the Australian government.

Paraguay
Status: Partly Free

LEGAL ENVIRONMENT: 13
POLITICAL INFLUENCES: 24
ECONOMIC PRESSURES: 18
TOTAL SCORE: 55

The constitution provides for freedom of the press, although the government does not always respect this right. Journalists covering strikes and protests risk intimidation and violent attacks by the security forces. In a country that is ranked as the most corrupt in Latin America, journalists also face considerable harassment and intimidation when reporting on corruption scandals. Media outlets and their owners sometimes face legal harassment through the courts as well. In December, a journalist was found guilty of defamation and ordered to pay large fines for an investigative story in which he allegedly "insulted the honor" of a prominent attorney and a former senator. Media independence is compromised by close relationships between the media and political parties and business. Nongovernmental media ownership is highly concentrated, and the economic situation in the country accentuates media dependency on political parties and big businesses for funding.

Peru

Status: Partly Free

LEGAL ENVIRONMENT: 9
POLITICAL INFLUENCES: 17
ECONOMIC PRESSURES: 9
TOTAL SCORE: 35

Status change explanation: Peru's rating slipped from Free to Partly Free in order to reflect some backsliding that has taken place under the Toledo government, including continuing legal intimidation and harassment of journalists.

The constitution provides for freedom of the press, but libel is a criminal offense and cases are frequently brought against journalists by politicians and other individuals. The media are diverse and present a wide spectrum of opinion. Since former president Alberto Fujimori's departure, both print and broadcast media have begun to show a balance in political coverage, although fear of legal proceedings and strong popular opinion discourages journalists from making pro-Fujimori statements. Despite this progress, there was some backsliding in press freedom during the year. Revelations of the scope and depth of media corruption under the Fujimori administration continue to affect public confidence in the media because of major media involvement in corruption and bribery. Journalists are subject to some harassment when covering the news, and during the year several received threats for reporting on corruption issues. As a result, there is some self-censorship. The practice of showing favoritism to media outlets through the awarding of advertising revenues has declined considerably, as has journalists' susceptibility to bribery, owing to strong public scrutiny.

Philippines

Status: Free

LEGAL ENVIRONMENT: 3
POLITICAL INFLUENCES: 17
ECONOMIC PRESSURES: 10
TOTAL SCORE: 30

Press freedom is provided for by law and is generally respected by the government. In November, free press advocates expressed concern that proposed antiterrorism legislation could impinge on freedom of expression. Although powerful families and businesses control many media outlets, the private press remains vigorous, though prone to innuendo and sensationalism. The greatest threats to journalists are continuing harassment, intimidation, and violence, which lead to some self-censorship. During 2002, two reporters were killed in apparent retaliation for their coverage of alleged corruption or for their criticism of local officials. Other journalists were abducted or threatened, and several radio stations were targeted for attack. Several past killings of journalists remain unsolved.

Poland

Status: Free

LEGAL ENVIRONMENT: 6
POLITICAL INFLUENCES: 5
ECONOMIC PRESSURES: 7
TOTAL SCORE: 18

Articles 14, 54, and 213 of the constitution ban censorship and provide guarantees for freedom of the press, and the media generally enjoy these rights in practice. With some gaps in enforcement, a 2001 law on freedom of information has noticeably improved access to official documents. Nevertheless, reporters continue to face the threat of imprisonment for libel against the state and public officials. In recent years, critical journalists have increasingly become the targets of politically motivated defamation suits. While self-censorship does exist, larger media organizations are willing to voice criticism. In February, authorities seized the passports of three executives at Presspublica, the publisher of the influential newspaper *Rzeczpospolita*, and placed the individuals under surveillance. Press freedom advocates noted that the government owned 49 percent of Presspublica and was likely trying to exert inappropriate influence over the management. The government controls four national television stations and four national radio broadcasters. Public broadcasters have demonstrated a marked dependence on the state, as partisan politicians retain a measurable amount of influence over content. In March, Prime Minister Leszek Miller introduced legislation that would benefit state media at the expense of private media groups. The draft bill prohibits private companies from owning both print and broadcast outlets but exempts government controlled media from any such restrictions. The law did not enter into force by the end of the year.

Portugal

Status: Free

LEGAL ENVIRONMENT: 5
POLITICAL INFLUENCES: 4
ECONOMIC PRESSURES: 6
TOTAL SCORE: 15

The constitution provides strong protections for freedom of the press, and the High Authority for the Media upholds the principles of a free and independent press. Laws prohibit insults against the government or the armed forces, although they are rarely enforced. In 2002, a Portuguese court ruled that authorities could bring charges against a journalist for refusing to reveal confidential sources in a criminal case. Most media outlets are independent of the government; however, print and broadcast ownership is concentrated in the hands of four main media companies.

Qatar

Status: Not Free

LEGAL ENVIRONMENT: 16
POLITICAL INFLUENCES: 24
ECONOMIC PRESSURES: 21
TOTAL SCORE: 61

The law does not provide for freedom of the press, and there are criminal penalties and jail sentences for libel. Despite the government's lifting official censorship on the media in 1995, because of social and political pressures, journalists continue to practice self-censorship when reporting on government policies, the ruling family, or neighboring states. However, general scrutiny of the government and its policies is common and tolerated. The five daily newspapers are all privately owned, but board members and owners either are government officials or have ties to the government. Qatar is the home of satellite news giant Al-Jazeera, which became well known around the world for its reporting in the aftermath of the attacks of September 11, 2001 on the United States. Although Al-Jazeera's critical coverage has angered a number of Arab regimes, the station tends to shy away from covering sensitive political issues within Qatar. In October, the Supreme Court sentenced a Jordanian journalist to death after convicting him of espionage. The International Federation of Journalists has expressed fears that the trial was unfair and that the punishment is an attempt to silence journalists.

Romania

Status: Partly Free

LEGAL ENVIRONMENT: 12
POLITICAL INFLUENCES: 14
ECONOMIC PRESSURES: 12
TOTAL SCORE: 38

Press freedom declined slightly in 2002 as a result of new legislation on access to information and continued political influence over state media. Article 30 of the constitution bans censorship and guarantees freedom of the press. At times, the government has acted to restrict these rights in practice. The penal code threatens journalists with imprisonment or fines for libel and insult. There are currently more than 300 such cases pending against journalists. In 2002, media and human rights organizations expressed concern over the passage of the Law on Classified Information. The law exempts several government agencies from public oversight and undermines sections of the 2001 Freedom of Information Act. The 2002 Audiovisual Law, intended to reform the broadcast sector, maintains the government's strict control over the distribution of television and radio licenses. Many media outlets are financially dependent on the government and reluctant to voice criticism. In one example, the largest private television station, Pro TV, owes the state nearly $50 million in unpaid taxes and relies heavily upon the good graces of the government for survival. No fewer than 1,500 private newspapers and magazines compete for Romanian readers. All but two television and radio stations are privately owned.

Russia
Status: Not Free

LEGAL ENVIRONMENT: 14
POLITICAL INFLUENCES: 30
ECONOMIC PRESSURES: 22
TOTAL SCORE: 66

Status change explanation: Russia's rating declined from Partly Free to Not Free because of the closure of the last independent national television broadcaster, negative state influence over public and private media, and repeated attacks against journalists.

Freedom of the press declined in Russia as a result of continued legal, political, and economic pressure. Article 29 of the constitution bans censorship and guarantees freedom of expression. However, Russian media do not always enjoy these rights in practice. Following critical reporting of the Moscow hostage crisis, parliament passed a law restricting media coverage of emergency or national security operations. President Vladimir Putin subsequently vetoed controversial sections of the law; however, the affair did little to diminish the growing antagonism between the government and the independent press. Prominent reporters and nongovernmental organizations have complained of an official campaign against independent journalism under Putin's "guided democracy." Journalists and media organizations are frequently the targets of politically motivated libel suits. Political influence permeates nearly all levels of the media. In January, judicial authorities ordered the closing of TV-6, the last independent national broadcaster, after a suit was brought against it by the partially state-owned energy company LUKoil. State-controlled broadcasters now dominate the national airwaves. The majority of newspapers and magazines are privately owned, yet a handful of powerful oligarchs control nearly all of the country's national publications. Journalists routinely experience harassment, physical violence, and death threats. The Committee to Protect Journalists reported that three media professionals were killed in connection with their work during 2002. The Russian military restricts access to the Chechen war zone, issuing accreditation primarily to those loyal to the government. The disruptive effects of the war severely hinder news production and the flow of information to the general public.

Rwanda

Status: Not Free

Legal Environment: 24
Political Influences: 33
Economic Pressures: 23
Total Score: 80

Citing the contentious and provocative role of certain media outlets during the 1994 genocide, the present government sharply restricts the ability of the media to operate freely. In December 2001, however, President Paul Kagame vetoed a media bill passed by the parliament in September that prescribed the death penalty for journalists found guilty of inciting genocide and would have compelled reporters to reveal confidential sources. The state continues to monopolize the broadcast media, although a media bill passed in June paved the way for the licensing of private radio and TV stations. There are a growing number of independent newspapers, but fearing official reprisals, many journalists practice self-censorship and coverage tends to follow the government line. Reporters continued to suffer intimidation, arbitrary arrest and detention, and deportation at the hands of authorities. The government is also able to influence the press through its purchase of advertising space, upon which many private publications are financially dependent.

Saint Kitts and Nevis

Status: Free

Legal Environment: 4
Political Influences: 7
Economic Pressures: 7
Total Score: 18

Press freedom is provided for in the constitution, the media are critical, and opposition newspapers freely scrutinize the government. There are no daily newspapers; however, the two major political parties publish weekly or fortnightly newspapers and there is a third, nonpartisan, weekly newspaper. The government owns and operates the major radio station and the only television station. State-run media outlets have been criticized for not adequately covering opposition rallies or providing opposition parties with equal media access.

Saint Lucia

Status: Free

LEGAL ENVIRONMENT: 0
POLITICAL INFLUENCES: 4
ECONOMIC PRESSURES: 4
TOTAL SCORE: 8

Citizens enjoy a high degree of press freedom, and there are no laws that restrict journalists and their work. The media carry a wide spectrum of views and are often critical of the government. Media outlets in the country are largely independent. There are five privately owned newspapers, two privately held radio stations, and one partially government-funded radio station, as well as two privately owned television stations.

Saint Vincent and the Grenadines

Status: Free

LEGAL ENVIRONMENT: 2
POLITICAL INFLUENCES: 8
ECONOMIC PRESSURES: 7
TOTAL SCORE: 17

Freedom of expression is provided for by the constitution, and there are no laws that restrict press freedom in the country. Two major newspapers and numerous smaller, partisan publications are all privately owned, and they openly scrutinize government policies. The only television station is privately owned and free from government interference. However, the country's sole radio station is state-owned and the government controls programming and also prohibits call-in shows. Some individual journalists have complained that government advertising, a significant source of revenue, is sometimes withheld from newspapers that are more critical of the government.

Samoa

Status: Free

LEGAL ENVIRONMENT: 4
POLITICAL INFLUENCES: 4
ECONOMIC PRESSURES: 16
TOTAL SCORE: 24

Samoa's press is generally free, though it is subject to some official harassment. A 1998 law enables government ministers to use public funds to finance defamation suits, and several have filed lawsuits against the *Samoa Observer*, an independent newspaper, over stories on alleged official corruption and abuses of power. Authorities also withdrew all government advertisements from the paper and threatened to cancel its business license. Two English-language newspapers and several Samoan-language papers appear regularly. The government runs the sole domestic television station, although satellite television is easily available. Radio is both public and private. In December, the opposition accused the state media of failing to cover its views.

San Marino

Status: Free

LEGAL ENVIRONMENT: 1
POLITICAL INFLUENCES: 3
ECONOMIC PRESSURES: 5
TOTAL SCORE: 9

The media are free in principle and practice, and existing laws protect freedom of expression and the press. During 2002, there were no reported violations of press freedom. The government, some political parties, and trade unions all publish newspapers. Italian print media and television broadcasts are freely available throughout the country. State-sponsored San Marino RTV operates both a radio and television station. Radio Titano is the country's sole privately owned radio station.

Sao Tome and Principe

Status: Free

LEGAL ENVIRONMENT: 1
POLITICAL INFLUENCES: 3
ECONOMIC PRESSURES: 15
TOTAL SCORE: 19

Constitutionally protected freedom of expression is respected in practice. There are no legal restraints on the media, which are also free from official intimidation or pressure. One state-run and six independent newspapers and newsletters are published sporadically. While the state controls a local press agency and the only radio and television stations, no law forbids independent broadcasting. Opposition parties receive free airtime, and newsletters and pamphlets scrutinizing the government circulate freely.

Saudi Arabia

Status: Not Free

LEGAL ENVIRONMENT: 29
POLITICAL INFLUENCES: 28
ECONOMIC PRESSURES: 23
TOTAL SCORE: 80

The authorities do not permit criticism of Islam or the ruling family, and direct criticism of the government is rare. A media policy statement and a national security law prohibit the dissemination of criticism of the government, though there is some leeway to scrutinize governmental bodies and social policies. Officially, journalists are urged to uphold Islam, oppose atheism, promote Arab interests, and preserve the cultural heritage of the country. Official censorship is common, as is self-censorship. Journalists must be licensed in order to practice their profession. The government tightly controls the entry of foreign journalists through the granting of visas. The Internet is widely available, but highly censored for content and monitored by authorities. Satellite television—through which Saudi citizens have access to news programs such as those of Al-Jazeera and CNN—is widespread, despite its illegal status. The government owns all broadcast media. Print media are privately owned although highly dependent on the state for funding.

Senegal

Status: Partly Free

LEGAL ENVIRONMENT: 15
POLITICAL INFLUENCES: 14
ECONOMIC PRESSURES: 9
TOTAL SCORE: 38

Although the government generally respects the constitutional provisions for freedom of expression and the press, it does occasionally impose some limits on these rights. A restrictive press law that prohibits "discrediting the state" and disseminating "false news" has been used to prosecute a number of journalists. In April, Mamadou Oumar Ndiaye, the publications director of the weekly *Le Temoin*, was sentenced to four months in jail for defamation. While the threat of legal penalties has resulted in some self-censorship, the private print and broadcast media are often highly critical of the government and political parties. Reporters continued to be subjected to some harassment at the hands of police. For example, it was not unusual for journalists to be detained for questioning and pressured to reveal confidential sources. Several reporters working in the Casamance region received death threats from separatist rebels in September.

Seychelles

Status: Partly Free

LEGAL ENVIRONMENT: 17
POLITICAL INFLUENCES: 16
ECONOMIC PRESSURES: 17
TOTAL SCORE: 50

The constitution provides for freedom of speech, but also protects the reputation, rights, and privacy of citizens, as well as the interests of public safety, order, morality, and health, which could potentially restrict reporting. Civil libel lawsuits resulting in steep monetary penalties have been used repeatedly against the independent media. In February, the weekly *Regar* was ordered to pay exorbitant damages in the latest of a series of lawsuits. Although the private press continues to criticize the government, some self-censorship persists. The state retains a near monopoly over the broadcast media, whose coverage adheres closely to official policy positions. High licensing fees have discouraged the development of privately owned broadcast media.

Sierra Leone

Status: Not Free

LEGAL ENVIRONMENT: 17
POLITICAL INFLUENCES: 26
ECONOMIC PRESSURES: 18
TOTAL SCORE: 61

Freedom of speech and of the press is guaranteed in the constitution, but the government at times restricts these rights. Criminal libel laws provided for in the Public Order Act are occasionally used to jail journalists. In November, Paul Kamara, the founding editor of *For Di People*, was convicted on 18 counts of libel, sentenced to nine months in jail, and ordered to pay a fine, while the court recommended that his newspaper be banned for six months. The Independent Media Commission, established by an act of parliament and charged with registering media outlets and regulating their conduct, suspended a newspaper in March and denied a broadcasting license to a private radio station in September. Dozens of newspapers are printed in Freetown, the capital, but most are of poor quality and often carry sensational or undocumented stories. Many openly criticize the government and armed factions. Several state-owned and private radio and television stations broadcast and remain an important source of public information. Corruption and bribe taking among poorly paid journalists continue to be problems. Reporters sometimes face harassment and intimidation at the hands of security forces.

LEGAL ENVIRONMENT: 24

POLITICAL INFLUENCES: 21

Singapore

ECONOMIC PRESSURES: 21

Status: Not Free

TOTAL SCORE: 66

The constitution provides for freedom of speech and expression but also permits restrictions on these rights. Although not used against the press in recent years, the Internal Security Act allows the government to restrict publications that incite violence, arouse racial or religious tension, or threaten national interests, national security, or public order. Legal constraints on the press also include harsh defamation laws, which several members of the government have successfully used to sue their critics. In July, a judge ruled that the courts could force journalists to reveal their sources in civil cases. The Newspaper and Printing Presses Act allows authorities to restrict the circulation of any foreign periodical that publishes an article allegedly interfering in domestic politics. In 2001 new legislation extended this provision to cover foreign broadcast services. International newspapers and magazines are available, although authorities have at times banned or censored foreign publications that carried articles the government found offensive. The privately held Singapore Press Holdings, which owns all general-circulation newspapers, has close ties to the ruling party. Government-affiliated agencies operate almost all broadcast media outlets, as well as Internet service providers and cable television services. As a result of legal pressures as well as the influence of owners over editorial content, many reporters practice self-censorship.

LEGAL ENVIRONMENT: 9

POLITICAL INFLUENCES: 6

Slovakia

ECONOMIC PRESSURES: 6

Status: Free

TOTAL SCORE: 21

Article 26 of the constitution bans censorship and provides for freedom of the press. Local media outlets generally enjoy these rights in practice. However, the media remain vulnerable to criminal libel laws and political interference. In 2002, the Constitutional Court suspended some sections of the criminal code relating to defamation of parliament and the state; other sections remain in effect and threaten journalists with harsh penalties for libel. Reporters are often the targets of politically motivated libel suits. During the 2002 parliamentary campaign, state and private television generally respected laws regarding objective political coverage. However, the state Office of Press and Information did cite the private *TV Markiza* for biased reporting. Private media are generally free from direct government interference, although powerful business interests somewhat limit editorial independence. The public broadcast sector remains financially and politically dependent upon the government.

Slovenia

LEGAL ENVIRONMENT: 3
POLITICAL INFLUENCES: 6
ECONOMIC PRESSURES: 10

Status: Free

TOTAL SCORE: 19

Article 39 of the constitution guarantees freedom of expression and the press. The media generally enjoy these rights in practice. However, libel remains a criminal offense, and the civil code prohibits insults against government officials. At times, journalists are the targets of politically motivated lawsuits. The press is generally independent of direct state interference. Nevertheless, self-censorship and various forms of political or editorial pressure continue to exist. In April, journalists at the state-run Radio-Televizija Slovenija (RTVS) threatened to strike over allegations of managerial censorship. The news director resigned soon after. With three radio stations and two television networks, RTVS is the single largest broadcaster in the country. There are four national commercial television stations and more than 60 independent radio stations. All newspapers are privately owned. Journalists occasionally experience harassment and physical violence in connection with their work. A notable example occurred in February 2001, when unknown individuals brutally assaulted *Vecer* newspaper reporter Miro Petek. The case remains unsolved, and parliament has opened a special commission to investigate the possibility of involvement by public officials.

LEGAL ENVIRONMENT: 3
POLITICAL INFLUENCES: 11
Solomon Islands
ECONOMIC PRESSURES: 11
Status: Free   TOTAL SCORE: 25

Press freedom is provided for in the constitution and is generally respected. The most important source of information is the state-run Solomon Islands Broadcasting Corporation (SIBC), which offers balanced coverage but occasionally comes under pressure from the government for airing opposition viewpoints. Three private newspapers vigorously scrutinize official policies. During the year, journalists faced some harassment. Armed supporters of a government minister forced the independent *Solomon Star* to pay him "compensation" for publishing an unflattering story in February, and in May SIBC staff were threatened by a group of militants, who also damaged equipment at the radio station.

LEGAL ENVIRONMENT: 23
POLITICAL INFLUENCES: 35
Somalia
ECONOMIC PRESSURES: 22
Status: Not Free   TOTAL SCORE: 80

The Transitional Charter, as well as the constitutions of Somalia's autonomous regions, provides for press freedom, but this right is sharply restricted in practice, mainly because of continuing political instability and the inability of the Transitional National Government to effectively assert its authority over the country. The government launched its first radio station, Radio Mogadishu, in 2001, while private print and broadcast media have been rejuvenated in the last several years. Some, such as the HornAfrik radio and television stations, provide balanced and independent coverage, but many outlets are linked to the various warlords and political factions. In May, regional authorities withdrew the broadcasting license of a company in Puntland, and in June the Somaliland government banned all privately owned radio stations. Reporters continue to face harassment, arbitrary arrest, and detention in all areas of the country, and a number have been forced into exile. In October, journalists went on strike to protest the passing of a harsh new media bill by the parliament. Shortly thereafter, the president refused to sign the bill into law, and at year's end, it was being redrafted with assistance from lawyers and journalists.

South Africa

Status: Free

LEGAL ENVIRONMENT: 6
POLITICAL INFLUENCES: 9
ECONOMIC PRESSURES: 10

TOTAL SCORE: 25

Freedom of expression and the press is protected in the constitution and is generally respected. However, several apartheid-era laws that remain in effect permit authorities to restrict the publication of information about the police, national defense forces, and other institutions, while the Criminal Procedure Act compels journalists to reveal sources. A variety of private newspapers and magazines are sharply critical of the government, political parties, and other societal actors. Radio broadcasting has been dramatically liberalized, with scores of small community radio stations now operating. The state-owned South African Broadcasting Corporation (SABC) is today far more independent than during apartheid, but still suffers from self-censorship. Press freedom groups expressed concern that provisions in the proposed Broadcasting Amendment Bill could further impinge on the editorial independence of the SABC. Reporters continue to be subjected to occasional instances of threats and harassment.

Spain

Status: Free

LEGAL ENVIRONMENT: 1
POLITICAL INFLUENCES: 8
ECONOMIC PRESSURES: 7

TOTAL SCORE: 16

The constitution guarantees freedom of expression and the press. The media enjoy these rights in practice; however, terrorist violence against journalists remains a lingering threat to press freedom. The Basque Fatherland and Liberty (ETA) movement has branded many journalists "traitors" for declining to support the group's nationalist ideology. In the past two years, several media professionals have died from alleged ETA letter bombs and assassinations. In January 2002, law enforcement officials acted to prevent letter bomb attacks against leading figures at the Correo Press Group, Radio Nacional de Espana, and Antena 3 television. Despite such threats, the country continues to maintain a vibrant media environment. The majority of print and broadcast media outlets are privately owned. The public has access to more than 100 newspapers covering a wide range of perspectives.

Sri Lanka

Status: Partly Free

LEGAL ENVIRONMENT: 11
POLITICAL INFLUENCES: 27
ECONOMIC PRESSURES: 14
TOTAL SCORE: 52

Status change explanation: Sri Lanka's rating improved from Not Free to Partly Free as a result of a cease-fire and continuing peace talks between the government and rebels, which facilitated a more open environment for the media, as well as the removal of criminal defamation legislation.

Although the constitution provides for freedom of expression, the government has restricted this right in practice, particularly with regard to coverage of the civil war. However, authorities lifted censorship of military-related news last year. The Liberation Tigers of Tamil Eelam (LTTE) rebel group tightly restricts the media in areas under its control. In a major advance for press freedom, an act of parliament removed criminal defamation legislation from the statute books in June. The government controls many of the largest media outlets, and political coverage in the state-owned media favors the ruling party. While private newspapers and broadcasters scrutinize government policies, journalists do practice some self-censorship. Reporters, particularly those who cover human rights issues, corruption, or police misconduct, continued to face some harassment, threats, and violent attacks at the hands of the police, security forces, government supporters, and the LTTE during the year. In February, a court sentenced two air force officers to prison terms for an attack on a journalist that had occurred four years ago. However, the murder of a BBC reporter in October 2000 by unidentified gunmen remains unsolved.

Sudan

Status: Not Free

LEGAL ENVIRONMENT: 26
POLITICAL INFLUENCES: 35
ECONOMIC PRESSURES: 23
TOTAL SCORE: 84

The government continues to severely restrict the ability of the media to operate freely despite constitutional provisions for freedom of expression. On the basis of national security legislation, authorities are empowered to conduct prepublication censorship, confiscate or ban publications, and detain journalists. The quasi-official National Press Council is responsible for applying the press law and has the power to license and suspend newspapers. Under the penal code, propagating false news is punishable by either a prison term or a fine. In January, Nhial Bol, the editor of the English-language daily *Khartoum Monitor,* was fined for publishing an article implicating the government in slavery. A number of Arabic- and English-language newspapers publish regularly and provide a variety of viewpoints and occasional criticism of the regime. All are subject to official censorship, and many journalists practice self-censorship in order to avoid harassment. Reporters Sans Frontieres noted that authorities had censored the independent media more than a dozen times during the year, often by seizing copies of the newspapers directly from the printing press. Journalists were also subjected to arrest, interrogation, and detention by the security forces as a result of their reporting. Broadcast media are directly controlled by the government and must reflect official views.

Suriname

Status: Free

LEGAL ENVIRONMENT: 0
POLITICAL INFLUENCES: 12
ECONOMIC PRESSURES: 14
TOTAL SCORE: 26

Freedom of the press is provided for in the constitution, and the government generally respects this right. There are no laws that restrict press freedom, though journalists do practice self-censorship on issues concerning human rights abuses that took place during the military dictatorship of Desi Bouterse. A few incidents involving the intimidation and harassment of journalists were reported during the year. Two daily newspapers, a dozen television stations, and many radio stations operate in several languages, reflecting the diversity of the population. The state places relatively high costs on establishing media outlets, and the media are somewhat reliant on the state for funding.

Swaziland

Status: Not Free

LEGAL ENVIRONMENT: 23
POLITICAL INFLUENCES: 26
ECONOMIC PRESSURES: 25
TOTAL SCORE: 74

Freedom of expression is seriously restricted, especially regarding political issues or matters concerning the royal family. Legislation bans the publication of any criticism of the monarchy, and journalists are occasionally prosecuted on criminal defamation charges. As a result, self-censorship is widely practiced. Journalists at Swaziland's only independent daily reported that they have trouble gaining access to official information. The government controls most broadcast media and finances a daily newspaper; it discourages critical news coverage at these outlets. However, broadcast and print media from South Africa are available. Reporters continued to be subjected to some intimidation and physical harassment at the hands of police and security forces. The government withholds advertising from the independent press and occasionally proscribes publications without providing adequate justification.

Sweden
Status: Free

LEGAL ENVIRONMENT: 1
POLITICAL INFLUENCES: 2
ECONOMIC PRESSURES: 5
TOTAL SCORE: 8

Legal protections for press freedom date back to the 1766 Freedom of the Press Act. Existing legislation protects confidential sources and access to official information. The state provides subsidies to support financially struggling newspapers. While such payments constitute just 3 percent of the national print revenue, they account for a quarter of the annual income for some local or regional papers. The majority of print and electronic outlets are privately owned. However, radio and television ownership is highly concentrated. Political divisions have limited parliamentary attempts to address the issue.

Switzerland
Status: Free

LEGAL ENVIRONMENT: 2
POLITICAL INFLUENCES: 3
ECONOMIC PRESSURES: 5
TOTAL SCORE: 10

Switzerland has an open and free media environment. Articles 16 and 94 of the Swiss Federal Constitution provide the legal basis for freedom of expression and the press. The penal code prohibits racist or anti-Semitic speech. In November, Switzerland's highest court placed a temporary ban on the sale of a book alleging ties between Osama bin

Laden's half-brother, a Swiss national, and al-Qaeda terrorists. Large media conglomerates are consolidating the newspaper industry and forcing the closure of small and medium-sized papers. The public Swiss Broadcasting Corporation dominates the radio and television sectors. With some exceptions, market forces generally limit private stations to local and regional broadcasts.

Syria

Status: Not Free

LEGAL ENVIRONMENT: 25
POLITICAL INFLUENCES: 33
ECONOMIC PRESSURES: 22
TOTAL SCORE: 80

The government strictly controls the dissemination of information and permits no written or oral criticism of the president, the ruling Ba'ath Party, the military, or the legitimacy of the government. The Emergency Law and penal code allow the government broad discretion in determining what constitutes illegal expression and prohibit the publishing of "inaccurate" information. Journalists found guilty of publishing such information are subject to prison terms and stiff fines. In 2001, the government amended its press law to allow publications that were circulated before 1963 to be reestablished, which led to a few privately owned newspapers being published during the year. State security services are known to detain and threaten local journalists as well as revoke credentials for reporting on sensitive topics, although not as frequently as in the past. Many journalists practice self-censorship to avoid a government reaction. The government owns the country's radio and television stations as well as the newspaper publishing houses. In 2002, conditions were set out for licensing private, commercial, FM radio stations, but these stations would not be able to broadcast news or political content. The government-controlled press has, however, increased its coverage of official corruption and governmental inefficiency. Satellite television is widely available and cuts across socioeconomic lines.

LEGAL ENVIRONMENT: 9
POLITICAL INFLUENCES: 8

Taiwan
ECONOMIC PRESSURES: 7

Status: Free
TOTAL SCORE: 24

The constitution provides for freedom of the press. Laws barring Taiwanese from advocating communism or independence from China remain on the books. However, these laws, along with penalties for libel, defamation, and insult, are not generally used to restrict journalists' coverage. A wide range of privately owned newspapers report aggressively on corruption and other sensitive issues and carry outspoken editorials. However, in March, authorities raided the offices of *Taiwan Next* and confiscated 160,000 copies of its latest issue, accusing the weekly magazine of endangering national security. Broadcast television stations are subject to some political influence by their shareholders, who include local governments, political parties, and the armed forces. Though it has refused to license private islandwide radio stations, the government has in recent years issued more than two dozen licenses for private regional stations.

LEGAL ENVIRONMENT: 26
POLITICAL INFLUENCES: 26

Tajikistan
ECONOMIC PRESSURES: 24

Status: Not Free
TOTAL SCORE: 76

Press freedom in Tajikistan registered slight gains during 2002. Article 30 of the constitution bans censorship and guarantees freedom of the press. However, the media do not enjoy these rights in practice. Under the penal code, journalists face harsh fines and imprisonment for libel and defamation of the president. As a consequence, self-censorship is widespread. The government holds regular "guidance" sessions for journalists in order to direct the nature and substance of reporting. There are no daily newspapers in the country. State-run publishing houses often refuse to print independent newspapers with content deemed off-limits by authorities. State broadcasters dominate the airwaves and offer flattering coverage of the government. Nevertheless, in a positive development, Asia-Plus initiated the capital's first private radio broadcast after the government lifted the ban on independent radio. The private station TV Service also began independent television broadcasts in Dushanbe, the capital. In June, the state dropped sedition charges against the exiled editor of the opposition newspaper *Charogi Ruz.*

Tanzania

Status: Partly Free

LEGAL ENVIRONMENT: 18
POLITICAL INFLUENCES: 16
ECONOMIC PRESSURES: 13
TOTAL SCORE: 47

Although the constitution provides for freedom of speech, several other laws limit the ability of the media to function effectively. Authorities are empowered to register and ban newspapers under the Newspaper Registration Act, while the Broadcasting Services Act provides for state regulation of the electronic media and the National Security Act allows the government to control the dissemination of information to the public. In May, independent journalist George Maziku faced criminal defamation charges after writing an article that allegedly "misrepresented" the intentions of parliament. Under the island of Zanzibar's separate and more restrictive media policies, journalists must be licensed and the state tightly controls the broadcast media. However, in December, journalists launched the weekly *Dira*, Zanzibar's first private newspaper. Reporters continue to face some harassment at the hands of authorities, particularly in Zanzibar, and a number practice self-censorship. Nevertheless, independent media outlets as well as the state-owned newspaper criticize official policies, although the government occasionally pressures outlets to suppress unfavorable stories. Despite the high costs associated with establishing new broadcast media, dozens of private radio stations have been established in recent years.

Thailand

Status: Partly Free

LEGAL ENVIRONMENT: 12
POLITICAL INFLUENCES: 12
ECONOMIC PRESSURES: 12
TOTAL SCORE: 36

Status change explanation: Thailand's rating declined from Free to Partly Free to reflect increased official pressure on both local and foreign media outlets throughout the year.

Media outlets were subject to increased pressure from Prime Minister Thaksin Shinawatra's administration in 2002. The constitution allows the government to restrict press freedom in order to preserve national security, maintain public order, or prevent insults to the royal family or Buddhism. Despite some progress in the redrafting of broadcasting laws, the 1941 Printing Act, which empowers authorities to shut down media outlets, remains in force. By law, radio stations must renew their licenses annually. The government and armed forces own or oversee most radio and broadcast television stations. Newspapers scrutinize official policies and report allegations of corruption and human rights abuses, but journalists exercise an increasing level of self-censorship. Editions of the *Far Eastern Economic Review* (FEER) and *The Economist* were banned early in the year, and in February the government threatened to deport two FEER reporters. According to the Thai Journalists Association, two editors were forced to resign and an independent media group's radio programs were taken off the air on the grounds that they were too critical of the government. Meanwhile, media organizations accused the government of intimidation after learning that an official anticorruption agency had been instructed to investigate the bank accounts of leading journalists and critical publications. Reporters, particularly in the provinces, were subjected to some harassment during the year.

Togo

Status: Not Free

LEGAL ENVIRONMENT: 26
POLITICAL INFLUENCES: 27
ECONOMIC PRESSURES: 21
TOTAL SCORE: 74

The media, already facing heavy legal restrictions as well as official harassment, came under increasing attack during 2002. The Press and Communication Code of 1998 declares in its first article that the media are free, but restricts press freedom in most of the 108 other articles. In September, the National Assembly passed an amendment to the code that increases the penalty for "defaming or insulting" the president, state institutions, courts, the armed forces, and public administration bodies to a jail term of one to five years. A number of journalists were arrested and sentenced to prison terms during the year on charges of defamation. Authorities regularly seize newspaper print runs, harass and detain reporters, and close media outlets. While the heavily politicized private print media regularly criticize official policies, independent broadcast media outlets offer little vibrant local news coverage or commentary. State-owned media outlets, including the only daily newspaper, the national television channel, and a number of radio stations, slant their coverage to favor the government. The financial viability of many independent publications is compromised by official pressure on advertisers as well as by police confiscations of print runs, both of which hinder sales. As a result, according to the Committee to Protect Journalists, reporters often accept bribes in exchange for giving favorable coverage.

Tonga
Status: Partly Free

LEGAL ENVIRONMENT: 12
POLITICAL INFLUENCES: 11
ECONOMIC PRESSURES: 9
TOTAL SCORE: 32

The independent press carries some scrutiny of government policies, although authorities and private individuals frequently file defamation suits against media outlets for airing critical statements. An editor and a reporter from the *Times of Tonga* are facing trial on defamation charges stemming from the publication of a letter claiming that the king had a secret bank account containing some $350 million. The independent newspaper's staff have faced a number of court actions over their reports. The print media consist of one government-owned weekly and several privately held publications. The broadcast media are both public and private. In a positive development, two journalists and a pro-democracy activist were awarded monetary damages in December for their wrongful imprisonment in 1996.

Trinidad and Tobago
Status: Free

LEGAL ENVIRONMENT: 4
POLITICAL INFLUENCES: 11
ECONOMIC PRESSURES: 10
TOTAL SCORE: 25

The constitution provides for freedom of speech and of the press, and the government generally respects this right in practice. In 2002, the turmoil that occurred after disputed elections took place in December 2001 came to an end with the ascendancy of the United People's

Movement. The new prime minister, Patrick Manning, has observed a hands-off policy regarding the media in contrast to his predecessor, Baseo Panday, who vehemently criticized the media during his tenure from 1995 to 2001. In September, Manning signed the Declaration of Chapultepec, bringing the island nation into a new era of press freedom. Former prime minister Panday had refused to sign the agreement because of what he called the media's "dissemination of lies, half-truths, and innuendos." There is a mix of state-owned and private media outlets. In the past, journalists have complained about the treatment of the media and limited access to government sources. There have also been complaints that the government as well as the business community has tried to control the press by withdrawing advertising funds. Many media outlets in the country are part of business conglomerates, which complicates the situation.

Tunisia

LEGAL ENVIRONMENT: 27
POLITICAL INFLUENCES: 28
ECONOMIC PRESSURES: 23

Status: Not Free

TOTAL SCORE: 78

Despite press code reforms in 2001, there was increased suppression of the media during the year. The press code and vaguely worded provisions prohibiting subversion and defamation stipulate high fines and long prison sentences for violators and are frequently used to intimidate the press. Although press freedom is provided for in the constitution, the government regularly interferes with this right. There are several independent newspapers and magazines; however, the government uses mandatory prescreening of publications to control the press and encourage self-censorship. The state maintains a monopoly on radio and television, which provide only official views. However, the public has access to foreign stations through satellite services. Although the Internet is available, official monitoring and censoring of the Internet ranks as one of the highest in the world. In June 2002, the founder of a satirical Internet site that provided a forum for opposition groups and politicians was arrested and sentenced to two years in prison for spreading "false information." Intimidation of journalists is widespread, and a number of detention and harassment cases were reported during the year. The government also uses archaic methods to control the press. One journalist who was recently released from prison after serving an 11-year sentence was banished to the south of the country. His refusal to comply led to his re-arrest. Newsprint subsidies and control of advertising revenues are used to encourage self-censorship.

Turkey

Status: Partly Free

LEGAL ENVIRONMENT: 23
POLITICAL INFLUENCES: 23
ECONOMIC PRESSURES: 9
TOTAL SCORE: 55

In 2002, state reforms designed to gain EU membership yielded some improvements in the areas of criminal libel law and minority-language broadcasting. Nevertheless, overall gains in press freedom remained stagnant during the year. Article 26 of the constitution guarantees freedom of the press. However, recent amendments restrict this right in the case of national security and classified information. The Anti-Terror Law prohibits separatist propaganda. The criminal code further prohibits insults against the state and incitement to violence. In 2002, the government limited the penalty for such acts to a maximum of three years' imprisonment. However, officials continue to strictly enforce these laws and journalists are frequently jailed for discussing the Kurds, the military, or political Islam. In August, parliament approved regulations allowing for Kurdish-language broadcasting. Yet, subsequent regulations restrict the number of hours for minority language programs and insist that all broadcasts take place on state-controlled stations. The government maintains a large degree of influence over both the public and private media.

Turkmenistan

Status: Not Free

LEGAL ENVIRONMENT: 30
POLITICAL INFLUENCES: 33
ECONOMIC PRESSURES: 29
TOTAL SCORE: 92

Turkmenistan's media are among the most tightly controlled in the world. Article 26 of the constitution provides for freedom of expression and access to information, but the authoritarian regime of President Saparmurat Niyazov flagrantly disregards these rights in practice. In general, the regime has attempted to quarantine the nation from outside information and uses the domestic mass media to advance the swelling cult of personality surrounding the president. The state exercises censorship over all print and electronic outlets. Access to foreign newspapers is severely restricted. Internet access is prohibitively expensive and subject to state control. In 2002, the government banned cable television and rooftop satellite dishes. The U.S.-funded Radio Liberty and the Russian Mayak radio station are some of the few alternative sources of news. Independent journalists are frequently beaten and harassed.

Tuvalu
Status: Free

LEGAL ENVIRONMENT: 0
POLITICAL INFLUENCES: 2
ECONOMIC PRESSURES: 14
TOTAL SCORE: 16

The constitution provides for press freedom, and this right is generally respected. All media are government-owned but provide balanced news coverage. They include Radio Tuvalu, the fortnightly *Tuvalu Echoes* newspaper, and a television station that broadcasts for several hours each day. Many Tuvaluans also pull in foreign television broadcasts on satellite dishes.

Uganda
Status: Partly Free

LEGAL ENVIRONMENT: 15
POLITICAL INFLUENCES: 16
ECONOMIC PRESSURES: 14
TOTAL SCORE: 45

The constitution provides for freedom of expression. However, several statutes require journalists to be licensed and meet certain standards, and a sedition law remains in force and has been used to prosecute journalists. In May, the Anti-Terrorism Act of 2002 was signed into law, providing a possible death sentence for anyone publishing news "likely to promote terrorism." Independent media outlets, including more than two dozen daily and weekly newspapers as well as a growing number of private radio and television stations, are often highly critical of the government and offer a range of opposition views. Nevertheless, *The Monitor*, a leading independent newspaper, was briefly closed in October over the veracity of a report regarding the government's fight against guerillas in the northern part of the country. Reporters continue to face some harassment and threats at the hands of both police and rebel forces. High annual licensing fees for radio and television stations place some financial restraints on the broadcast media.

Ukraine

	LEGAL ENVIRONMENT: 15
	POLITICAL INFLUENCES: 29
	ECONOMIC PRESSURES: 23
Status: Not Free	TOTAL SCORE: 67

Status change explanation: Ukraine's rating declined from Partly Free to Not Free because of state censorship of television broadcasts, continued harassment and disruption of independent media, and the failure of the authorities to adequately investigate attacks against journalists.

Freedom of the press declined under the continued weight of political pressure and government censorship. Article 34 of the constitution, and a 1991 law on print media, guarantee freedom of expression and the press, but journalists do not enjoy these rights in practice. Official influence and de facto censorship are widespread. The administration issues regular instructions (*temniks*) to mass media outlets directing the nature, theme, and substance of news reporting. The European Institute for the Media reported that coverage at the state broadcaster UT-1 clearly favored the ruling party during the March 2002 parliamentary campaign. Opposition media outlets face various forms of harassment, including obstructive tax audits, safety inspections, and selective enforcement of media regulations. Libel ceased to be a criminal offense in 2001; however, politically motivated civil suits are common. Journalists frequently experience physical assaults, death threats, and murder as a result of their work. In March 2002, Reporters Sans Frontieres noted that 10 journalists have died under suspicious circumstances in the past four years, while another 41 have suffered serious injury from attacks. In October, the body of Ukrainian News director Mykhailo Kolomyets was discovered in northwestern Belarus nearly a week after he had disappeared from Kyiv. Kolomyets's news agency had at times been critical of the government. The case remained open by year's end. The well-publicized murder of journalist Heorhiy Gongadze also remains unsolved. Although print and broadcast media are largely in private hands, the state maintains control over the central printing and distributing centers.

LEGAL ENVIRONMENT: 24
POLITICAL INFLUENCES: 27

United Arab Emirates

ECONOMIC PRESSURES: 23

Status: Not Free

TOTAL SCORE: 74

The constitution provides for freedom of the press. However, there is strong regulatory and political control over the media, as well as an unwritten yet generally recognized ban on criticism of the government. Self-censorship is widespread on the topics of government policy, national security, and religion. The broadcast media are almost entirely state-owned and offer only official viewpoints. Print media outlets are mostly privately owned but are heavily dependent on the state for funding. There were some reports of harassment and intimidation of journalists during the year. In 2002, a poet who wrote verses that called neighboring Saudi Arabia's Islamic judges corrupt and labeled the Saudi regime "tyrants" was jailed and the editor who published the poem was fired. Internet access is widespread, although the authorities censor pornographic and radical Islamic sites. Satellite television also offers unfettered access to international news sources.

LEGAL ENVIRONMENT: 6
POLITICAL INFLUENCES: 5

United Kingdom

ECONOMIC PRESSURES: 7

Status: Free

TOTAL SCORE: 18

The 1998 Human Rights Act provides a statutory right to freedom of expression (though limited by the European Convention, which includes exceptions for public safety, health, morals, and the reputation of others). The 2000 Freedom of Information Act grants access to significant areas of information previously closed to the press. The act excludes information related to national defense, international issues, commercial interests, and law enforcement. The media enjoy these rights in practice. However, journalists and media outlets are subject to strict libel and obscenity laws. Print media outlets are privately owned and independent, though many of the national daily newspapers are aligned with political parties. The BBC operates half the broadcast media, which are funded by the state but are editorially independent. Authorities may monitor Internet messages and e-mail without judicial permission in the name of national security and "well being." The murder of prominent Northern Ireland journalist Martin O'Hagan remained unsolved more than a year after his death.

United States of America

Status: Free

LEGAL ENVIRONMENT: 5
POLITICAL INFLUENCES: 6
ECONOMIC PRESSURES: 6
TOTAL SCORE: 17

Freedom of expression is guaranteed by the constitution, and this right is generally respected. Nevertheless, in July, a publisher and an editor in Kansas were convicted of criminal libel, a rarity in the United States although 19 states permit such prosecution. Official restrictions on domestic press coverage, begun after the September 11, 2001, terrorist attacks, were expanded in preparation for U.S. military action in Iraq. The U.S. attorney general placed further limits on information accessible under the Freedom of Information Act, which substantially increased the volume of classified government information. The Federal Bureau of Investigation was empowered to conduct surveillance on the Internet without a court order. While some journalists complained about heightened secrecy, others accepted war-related restrictions but feared that such restrictions also hid normal political and economic information unrelated to military needs. In a policy reversal, however, the Defense Department began training journalists to accompany frontline troops. During past military campaigns, the press was either banned from field coverage or closely "minded" by the military. The Federal Communications Commission (FCC) began considering further deregulation of broadcast media. For two decades, mergers and buyouts have steadily reduced the number of persons controlling the content of large media networks. The FCC's latest action could further diminish diversity by allowing more broadcast outlets to be linked to print media in the same city or region.

Uruguay
Status: Free

LEGAL ENVIRONMENT: 12
POLITICAL INFLUENCES: 7
ECONOMIC PRESSURES: 11
TOTAL SCORE: 30

The constitution provides for press freedom, and the media generally operate freely and are often critical of the government. Defamation, contempt, and libel are considered criminal offenses and are punishable by up to three years' imprisonment. Over the past year, press freedom has been threatened by a series of trials and lawsuits in the courts involving charges of libel, requiring journalists to reveal sources, or concerning the controversial right of reply. The courts frequently enforce the right of reply in favor of the prosecution, which some consider to be a flagrant form of censorship. In contrast, the Chamber of Deputies approved a bill that will allow public access to government documents and information. There were some cases in which harassment and intimidation of journalists occurred, most often in relation to the coverage of corruption scandals. Taxes continue to be a heavy burden on the print press, as is the very high cost of distribution. Some media outlets have accused government agencies of withholding advertising revenues from outlets that are critical of the government.

Uzbekistan
Status: Not Free

LEGAL ENVIRONMENT: 26
POLITICAL INFLUENCES: 36
ECONOMIC PRESSURES: 24
TOTAL SCORE: 86

Since the country's independence from the Soviet Union in 1991, the administration of President Islam Karimov has substantially impeded the development of a free press. Article 29 of the constitution guarantees freedom of expression and information, while Article 67 bans censorship. However, the media do not enjoy these rights in practice. In May, the state ended formal censorship of the press by shifting responsibilities directly to editors. The next month, administration officials set an example of noncompliance and removed the chief editor of the weekly newspaper *Mohiyat* following the publication of an article on press freedom. Other newspaper editors quickly hired former government censors to vet all material prior to publication. The result is the same as that which occurred under state-mandated censorship. Libel and defamation of the president remain criminal offenses. Critical journalists frequently experience harassment, death threats, and physical violence. Radio and television stations are subject to annual re-registration. The Karimov administration has used this process to revoke the licenses of unsympathetic broadcasters. The state controls all aspects of printing and distribution. The government dominates the main journalists' union, and there are no independent journalists associations.

Vanuatu

Status: Free

LEGAL ENVIRONMENT: 2
POLITICAL INFLUENCES: 5
ECONOMIC PRESSURES: 14
TOTAL SCORE: 21

The press is generally free, despite the previous government's controversial 2001 deportation of a leading newspaper publisher on the grounds that he had revealed state secrets in his reporting on alleged government corruption. The chief justice overturned the deportation within a week, and the journalist returned to Vanuatu and resumed his work. Though the government permits criticism of its policies on state-run broadcasting, individual politicians and their supporters occasionally verbally threaten the media. The government runs a weekly newspaper, two radio stations, and a television station that serves Port Vila, the capital. At least three private newspapers, one of them run by a political party, compete with the state media.

Venezuela

Status: Not Free

LEGAL ENVIRONMENT: 23
POLITICAL INFLUENCES: 29
ECONOMIC PRESSURES: 16
TOTAL SCORE: 68

Status change explanation: Venezuela's rating deteriorated from Partly Free to Not Free, as the ability of independent journalists and media outlets to operate freely and impartially was seriously impeded by a political and economic crisis that enveloped the entire country.

Press freedom has seriously deteriorated over the past year as a result of a climate of intimidation and hostility towards independent journalists and media outlets. Although the constitution provides for press freedom, a special clause which states that all persons have the right to "true" information has been used by the government of President Hugo Chavez to censor and intimidate the press. Libel and defamation are criminal offenses, and these laws were increasingly used to harass the media throughout the year. A 1994 law requires that media professionals hold a university degree in journalism and also be members of the National College of Journalists. The government has exerted undue pressure on the media, repeatedly singling out media owners, editors, and reporters by name and calling them "liars, enemies of the revolution and of the people." During the year, dozens of journalists were the victims of threats, intimidation, and violent assaults, most likely as a result of the president's relentless criticism of the media. One journalist was killed after he was shot by a military sniper while covering political demonstrations that led to the temporary ousting of Chavez in February. On the other hand, the media in Venezuela have shown a significant anti-Chavez slant that is characterized by lowered levels of impartiality and fairness. Media owners allege that this situation exists because Chavez incites his supporters to attack journalists. In addition, the state allocates broadcasting licenses in a biased manner and shows favoritism with government advertising revenues.

Vietnam

LEGAL ENVIRONMENT: 30
POLITICAL INFLUENCES: 30
ECONOMIC PRESSURES: 22

Status: Not Free

TOTAL SCORE: 82

The media, already tightly regulated by the ruling Communist Party, faced further government-imposed restrictions in 2002. Although the constitution guarantees press freedom, the criminal code contains broad national security and antidefamation provisions that restrict free speech. In addition, a 1999 law requiring journalists to pay damages to individuals or groups that have been harmed by press articles has been invoked in at least one lawsuit. In January, the government published a decree instructing police to confiscate and destroy prohibited publications. The Committee to Protect Journalists expressed concern in July over a number of official efforts to curtail access to information, including banning the public's access to satellite television broadcasts and clamping down on press coverage of a key corruption scandal. Authorities also further tightened controls over the Internet, blocking thousands of sites and requiring all owners of Internet cafes to submit to licensing and background checks. All media outlets are owned by the government, and many journalists practice self-censorship. A number of journalists and cyber-dissidents were arrested or detained during the year, and several were sentenced to lengthy prison terms for their writings.

Yemen

Status: Not Free

LEGAL ENVIRONMENT: 27
POLITICAL INFLUENCES: 24
ECONOMIC PRESSURES: 18
TOTAL SCORE: 69

Libel is a criminal offense punishable by fines, flogging, and up to five years in prison for ambiguous acts such as "humiliating the State" or publishing "false information." Extralegal government harassment has diminished; however, detentions, harassment, and intimidation continue to restrict press freedom. Foreign journalists were also subjected to intimidation through frequent government interrogations of journalists reporting on the national military and other sensitive topics. The government closed down at least three publications after they published articles that were critical of the state or neighboring countries, or for reporting on state security matters. Regulations stipulate that newspapers must apply annually to renew licenses to operate, which some critics claim is aimed at putting some opposition newspapers out of business. The government controls most of the printing presses, with only one newspaper having its own press. The government also provides subsidies to certain newspapers that are privately owned.

Yugoslavia (Serbia and Montenegro)

Status: Partly Free

LEGAL ENVIRONMENT: 10
POLITICAL INFLUENCES: 18
ECONOMIC PRESSURES: 12
TOTAL SCORE: 40

Despite some persistent obstacles, press freedom continued to improve in 2002. Articles 36 and 38 of the 1992 constitution guarantee freedom of expression and ban censorship. The media have generally enjoyed these rights during the post-Milosevic period. While the press is primarily free from direct state interference, public officials frequently use libel suits in retaliation for critical news coverage. Consequently, some journalists practice self-censorship. In July, the Serbian parliament approved the creation of a media oversight council. The new body will enforce broadcast regulations and issue frequency licenses. In November, the Montenegrin parliament approved the implementation of media reform legislation. While several groups and press associations welcomed the initiative, some expressed concern that the regulations will require editors to consult political parties about the content of articles and restrict the number of stories published about parties in the run-up to elections. In both Serbia and Montenegro, journalists continue to experience harassment, threats, and physical violence as a result of their work. Although there were no reported murders of media professionals during the year, the 1998 murder of *Dnevni Telegraf* editor in chief Slavko Curuvija and the 2001 murder of *Vecernje Novosti* reporter Milan Pantic remain unsolved.

Zambia

Status: Not Free

LEGAL ENVIRONMENT: 20
POLITICAL INFLUENCES: 24
ECONOMIC PRESSURES: 19
TOTAL SCORE: 63

Freedom of speech is constitutionally guaranteed, but the government often restricts this right. The Public Order Act, among other statutes, has at times been used to harass journalists. In addition, during the year the ruling party responded to critical coverage by charging several editors and reporters under harsh criminal libel laws, which provide for prison terms of up to three years. The private media supported the introduction of freedom of information, broadcasting, and independent broadcasting authority draft laws, which aim, respectively, to facilitate easier access to information held by official organs, to transform the state-owned Zambia National Broadcasting Corporation from a government propaganda organ to a public broadcaster, and to establish an independent regulator to regulate broadcasting. The government currently dominates broadcasting, although an independent radio station, Radio Phoenix, presents nongovernmental views. Coverage at state-owned media outlets is generally supportive of the government, and as a result of prepublication review at government-controlled newspapers, journalists commonly practice self-censorship. Reporters continued to face threats and physical assault at the hands of police and ruling party supporters, and newspaper vendors who sell critical publications were also attacked during the year. In April, a local press association condemned corruption and bribe taking, which it alleged were rife in both the state-owned and private media.

Zimbabwe

LEGAL ENVIRONMENT: 30
POLITICAL INFLUENCES: 34
ECONOMIC PRESSURES: 24

Status: Not Free

TOTAL SCORE: 88

Under President Robert Mugabe, freedom of the press continues to be severely limited. A range of restrictive legislation—including the Official Secrets Act, the Public Order and Security Act, and criminal defamation laws—have been broadly interpreted by authorities in order to prosecute journalists. In addition, the 2002 Access to Information and Protection of Privacy Act (AIPPA) gives the information minister sweeping powers to decide who can work as a journalist in Zimbabwe and requires all journalists to register with a government commission. It also criminalizes the publication of "inaccurate" information. By the end of the year, the act had been used to arrest at least a dozen journalists. However, its legality was challenged in court by a number of professional organizations. There are no privately owned broadcast media outlets, and just one independent daily newspaper, the *Daily News*, continues to operate. State-controlled radio, television, and newspapers are all seen as mouthpieces of the government and cover opposition activities only in a negative light. Independent media outlets and their staff are subjected to considerable verbal intimidation, physical attacks, arrest and detention, and financial pressure at the hands of the police, authorities, and supporters of the ruling party. Foreign correspondents based in the country, particularly those whose reporting portrayed the regime in an unfavorable light, were refused accreditation or threatened with lawsuits and deportation.

Freedom House Board of Trustees

About Freedom House

FREEDOM HOUSE is a clear voice for democracy and freedom around the world. By supporting democratic change, monitoring freedom, and advocating for democracy and human rights, Freedom House seeks to empower people, to open closed societies, and to assist countries in transition to democratic rule.

FOUNDED MORE than sixty years ago by Eleanor Roosevelt, Wendell Willkie, and other Americans concerned with the mounting threats to peace and democracy, Freedom House has been a vigorous proponent of democratic values and a steadfast opponent of dictatorships of the far left and the far right. Today, Freedom House is a leading advocate of the world's young democracies, which are coping with the legacies of statism, dictatorship, and political repression.

FREEDOM HOUSE conducts an array of U.S. and overseas research, advocacy, education, and training initiatives that promote human rights, democracy, free market economics, the rule of law, independent media, and U.S. engagement in international affairs. Wherever basic liberties are threatened or democracies are emerging, Freedom House is engaged.

To LEARN MORE about Freedom House, visit www.freedomhouse.org.